A B C
of Architecture

ABC
of Architecture

JAMES F. O'GORMAN

Drawings by Dennis E. McGrath

PENN

University of Pennsylvania Press

Philadelphia

Text copyright © 1998 James F. O'Gorman
Drawings copyright © 1998 Dennis E. McGrath
All rights reserved
Printed in the United States of America on acid-free paper

10 9 8 7 6 5 4

Published by
University of Pennsylvania Press
Philadelphia, Pennsylvania 19104-4011

Library of Congress Cataloging-in-Publication Data
O'Gorman, James F.
    ABC of architecture / James F. O'Gorman ; drawings by Dennis E. McGrath.
          p.   cm.
    Includes bibliographical references and index.
    ISBN 0-8122-3423-5 (cloth : alk. paper). — ISBN 0-8122-1631-8
(pbk. : alk. paper)
      1. Architecture.   I. Title.
NA2530.036   1997
720—dc21   97-22616
                                                                  CIP

Designed by Carl Gross

To the memory of

Professor Richard O'Gorman, 1928–1996

Rest easy, Bro'

CONTENTS

"The beginning of wisdom," according to a West African proverb, "is to get you a roof."

—Annie Dillard, *The Writing Life*

PREFACE

Teachers learn from their students. In more than three decades of teaching undergraduates in the liberal arts I have learned that architecture can be for them a deeply mysterious subject. There are exceptions, of course, but many students approach it with fear and misgiving, if not with fear and loathing. Most of them, especially those who major in art history, can handle the formal analysis of a painting or a piece of sculpture, and then pass on to its story, if it tells one, or its meaning, if it has one. Buildings can bewilder them. There are no "pictures"; there is, apparently, only geometry. They might be able to handle the formal analysis, if only they knew where to begin, if only they had the vocabulary. Many of them are unconscious of the fact that architecture is a form of communication, that a building conveys meaning.

The following is a primer, a brief introduction to architecture for the beginning undergraduate or educated amateur. I find the existing basic books too prolix: fine if you already know the subject; too lengthy, too labyrinthine, if you do not. As a primer this book is intended to provide a toehold on the subject. It contains a précis for those short on time and a more leisurely discussion for the armchair set. To avoid repetition, read one or the other.

"Incompetence will show in the use of too many words," according to Ezra Pound, whose *ABC of Reading* I discovered while working on this book. I have tried to keep that warning in mind. The reader wishing to move on from this slender toehold to a more substantial footing will find a few detailed or specialized books named in the reading list. They will carry the student to the next level.

I have briefly outlined the basic elements of architecture. I want to dispel the mystery surrounding the art of making buildings, so I have avoided the gobbledygook currently clouding discussions of the subject by grandstanding architects and their apologists. I claim no originality or completeness. My approach is grounded not in theory but experience, my long experience as a teacher introducing students to the process by which some of a society's needs become architecture. I hope I have provided a vehicle by means of which the inquisitive can reach a preliminary understanding of what goes into a building's design and construction, and what basic elements should be considered in describing, analyzing, or criticizing a work of architecture.

I must warn the architect and the builder that this is a text intended for the education of the client. It is for the layperson, not the professional. I will of course be happy if the expert finds merit here, but I will be happier if the student burrowing in the darkness of confusion and despair finds a ray of light glowing at the end of the tunnel. And I will be happiest if the fundamentals the student carries out of that tunnel make him or her more critically aware of the built environment, eager to move on to more advanced reading about architecture, and more ready to join the architect and the builder in giving it congenial shape.

PRÉCIS

An ancient Roman architect named Vitruvius wrote that a building must be considered "with due reference to function, structure, and beauty" (*Utilitas, Firmitas,* and *Venustas* in his original Latin). This is an exquisite formulation; for all its antiquity it remains a useful framework for the preliminary analysis of a building. Vitruvius gave us the ABC of architecture.

Architecture begins when a person or an institution has a problem that can be solved only by building. That person—the client—states his or her needs in a "building program." The architect interprets that program in drawings. The builder translates those drawings into the finished building.

There are three basic types of architectural drawings. The plan diagrams function; the section (in part) diagrams structure; the elevation evokes beauty (let us hope it does, anyway). The plan represents the client's needs; the section tells the builder what structure to use; plan, section, and above all elevation demonstrate the architect's design, his formal solution to the building program.

Think of the Vitruvian factors as the corners of an equilateral triangle, or better, the legs of a tripod called architecture. None can stand alone; each is dependent upon the other two to form the work of architecture. In the same way, client, builder, and architect, plan, section, and elevation, are all interdependent. To understand a work of architecture is to recognize this mutuality, to learn as much as you can about all three interactive factors.

You must first ask what kind of building you are studying. What did the client want? What did the building program require? The work of architecture is the result of the architect's interpretation of program in relation to the client's budget, the building's site, and the availability of materials and structural technology.

Next you must look at the plan as a diagram of the building's intended use, its function. If a drawing of the plan is not at hand you must reconstruct it from the building. This is as close as you can get to the building program—the statement of function—if it too is missing. The plan demonstrates the relationships between the items of the program that have spatial equivalents. A school, for example, will have classrooms, an auditorium, a gymnasium, corridors, restrooms, and so on.

Within the plan you will find that there are two kinds of spaces: primary and secondary. Primary spaces represent the main function of the building; secondary spaces make those primary spaces usable. For example, in the school, classrooms and auditorium are primary; corridors and restrooms are secondary. The architect will organize his or her diagram of function according to this hierarchy.

You will find that there are basically two kinds of plans: the additive and the divisive. The additive plan strings discrete rooms into a usually irregular pattern. The divisive plan separates spaces within a larger and usually simple perimeter. The additive plan is often asymmetrical. The divisive plan is often symmetrical. As we shall see, the one usually generates complex three-dimensional forms; the other, simple solid shapes.

Once the architect has diagrammed function, he or she begins to think in three dimensions. That means choosing a structural system. (In fact, although I must outline these procedures sequentially, the architect must consider all three of the Vitruvian factors simultaneously. As I said, they are interdependent.)

The architect and the builder have a choice between two basic structural systems: the trabeated and the arcuated. The former is based on a unit of two verticals (posts) supporting a horizontal (lintel). In three dimensions this becomes a rectangular frame. The latter is composed of wedge-shaped stones, or voussoirs, that arc between posts (if it is built of reinforced concrete there are no voussoirs, but the mechanics are similar). In three dimensions this becomes a vault or dome. The trabeated system creates a closed rectangle, although it can be opened by the use of cantilevers, or beams supported at midpoint with free or "floating" ends. The arcuated system generates diagonal thrusts, so it must be buttressed in one of several ways. Arch and buttress can form a pyramidal outline. As we know from the Golden Gate Bridge, there are also suspension structures. They occur less often, and so more dramatically, in buildings.

Whether trabeated, arcuated, or suspended, a structure seeks stasis by balancing forces in tension and compression. Tension pulls; compression pushes. They operate in opposite directions, and if they are not balanced they will destroy a building. You must ask, "In what way does the structure achieve stasis?" "What impact does the struggle of forces have on its plan, its overall form?"

Architecture first happened when someone thought it might be nice to get in out of the wet or cold, to create a usable interior space. Space is common to all the formal arts, but as a general rule painting represents space; sculpture displaces space; and architecture encloses space, usable space. Since structure creates space, the choice of trabeated or arcuated will determine the character of a building's interior. A room shaped by the post-and-lintel system will probably have a flat ceiling, for example; use of an arcuated system might result in a vaulted space. And of course, interior space (like plan) determines external form.

The architect creates beauty through formal design. Selection of structural system impacts upon plan (as the plan influences this selection), and it affects the form of a building's interior and thus its exterior as well. Depending on the architect's choice of plan type, additive or divisive, that exterior might be picturesque (irregular) or formal (regular).

A picturesque building is asymmetrical, dynamic, colorful, visually energetic. A formal building is symmetrical, quiet, usually monochromatic, decorous. Axial alignment plays no part in the picturesque work; the axis dominates the formal. In the former, doors and windows often assume irregular shapes and distribution; the skyline breaks into spires, towers, dormers, high roofs. Our usual diagonal approach emphasizes its irregularity. In the latter, openings of repetitive design occur evenly spaced, main doors are centered, a horizontal cornice or simple roof caps the building, and we usually approach it head-on so that its balance is obvious.

On the exterior—as in the interior—choice of materials is an important consideration in determining color, scale, weight, and other architectural values. Brick, stone, stucco, enameled metal panels, plate glass: each imparts its own effect upon the finished building.

The distribution of windows on the exterior is notable, as is their placement in relation to interiors. Color and light play important roles in the characterization of interior space as well as of exterior form. Direct or indirect, side or overhead, natural or artificial illumination determines the character of a design.

Beauty, architectural beauty, is the hoped-for result of appropriate planning and sturdy structure. But beauty is relative. The Vitruvian factors remain dependent on each other, but they change individually over time. We must now think of them in terms of history. Architecture and history go hand in hand.

Building types, and hence building programs, vary from era to era. The individual client represents society at large, and that means he or she represents the wants and wishes of a given period. The Renaissance wanted primarily churches and palaces. Not until the nineteenth century could a client order a railroad station or a public library; not until the twentieth might he or she need an air terminal.

The Greeks built with post and beam; the Romans added arches and vaults. These systems, the trabeated and the arcuated, were originally achieved in natural, masonry materials, and that meant a large investment of mass to create a relatively small amount of space. Ancient buildings look heavy, solid. With the coming of the Industrial Revolution and the production of lighter and stronger synthetic materials such as iron, steel, reinforced concrete, and plate glass, architects using the same systems could achieve larger spans and more spacious buildings. A Greek temple embodies a structural system in the same category as that of the Empire State Building; what differences they exhibit are functions of history.

Standards of beauty, or style, change over time. From the classicism of the Greeks and Romans to the Gothic of the Middle Ages, from the heavy-walled, sculpted forms of older buildings resting solidly on the ground to the delicate glazed buildings of the twentieth century that seem to dance over the earth on tiptoe, buildings have always reflected the society that ordered them, the technology available to build them, and the prevailing artistic theory that gave them shape.

Your study must ultimately tie the building into the historical era that created it. What style is it? To answer this you must read history: social, technological, and artistic history. No analysis is possible without the knowledge gained from such study.

Vitruvius tells us that the classical orders were modeled on the human body: the sturdy Doric a young man, the more delicate

Ionic a young woman, and so on. He suggests that architecture takes on meaning through metaphor. Architecture is a language of metaphor. The pointed arches of the Gothic suggest a Christian church; the dome of the U.S. Capitol communicates political power. Those meanings have their roots in history. You must learn to read architecture by reading history.

Finally, no analysis of a building is possible unless you have the right vocabulary. "That thing sticking out of the roof" won't do. If it's a chimney, call it that; if it's a dormer, call it that. If you don't know the correct term, use a dictionary. *The Penguin Dictionary of Architecture* is a handy choice, but there are many of them, and they are usually illustrated.

The analysis of a building studies plan, structure, and style in relation to historical period. There is nothing prescribed in this book about beauty, which is ultimately a relative standard. I might not like what you like. Aesthetic preference comes from outside the Vitruvian triad. In your judgment of the visual success or failure of the architect's solution to the task ordered by the client, you are on your own.

ARCHITECTURE

You are outside on a treeless plain. It is raining (or snowing). It is hot (or cold). You want shelter. You want to go *inside*.

The first person to act upon that wish invented architecture. That person created the original building program, recognized the first of a list of needs that could be satisfied only by building, because, although most of our celebrity architects have forgotten the fact, architecture first and foremost provides us with shelter from the elements. Before everything else buildings (should) keep us warm (or cool) and dry. A yurt or a cave, you say, will keep us warm and dry. The yurt and the cave are architectural forms, I reply, although here I am particularly concerned with monumental, permanent, manufactured buildings. Architecture is an art that begins by creating habitable interiors.

Architecture is more than mere shelter; it rises to the realm of art. It shares certain characteristics with other concrete art forms, especially painting and sculpture: abstract principles such as design, composition, form, light, color patterns, and so on. The great buildings, the monuments we can all agree stand at the top of the architectural pecking order, are great works of art. Few paintings or pieces of sculpture offer the aesthetic wallop of the atmosphere of the Court of the Lions at the Alhambra in Granada, the soaring interior of the cathedral at Beauvais, or the distant profile of Mont-Saint-Michel shimmering in the early morning mist off the coast of Normandy.

Architecture can be distinguished from the other arts by its fundamental property, its usable interior. Light and space are formative elements common to all the visual arts. It is obvious that light shapes form, that we need light to see form. How the painter, the sculptor, or the architect manipulates light determines the character

BEAUVAIS

of a work of art. It is the element of space, however, that sets architecture apart from the other arts. Painting, sculpture, and architecture all exist in space; each has a primary character related to space. Painting *represents* space (whether two- or three-dimensional); sculpture *displaces* space; architecture *encloses* space. It is true that some painting reaches for the third dimension, and it is true that some sculpture—Henry Moore's work comes immediately to mind—encompasses space. It is also true that in recent years some artists have tried to blur the distinctions between the arts—as others have tried to blur the differences between the genders. May neither attempt succeed. All generalizations have exceptions, but special cases do not concern us here. Architecture is in general distinguished from the other arts because it alone is primarily concerned with creating usable interior space.

Painted or sculpted space is purely aesthetic; architectural space is first of all utilitarian. Architectural art begins physical and ends psychological. Buildings spring from a basic need, our need for overhead shelter from the pouring rain or beating sun, and lateral enclosure against suffocating heat and intense cold. That need calls for a structural solution. It is satisfied by means of architectural statics, the balance of forces allowing the walls to rise beside us and the roof to span above us. These form the masses that enclose usable interior space. What shape those masses, or solids, take depends on a variety of factors, not the least of which are artistic theory and style. This architectural triad—of need, means, and art— has since antiquity constituted the ABC of architecture.

A Roman republican architect and engineer, Marcus Vitruvius Pollio, wrote what, through the accidents of historical survival, became the only book on architecture we have inherited from classical antiquity. It is the oldest, and probably the most influential, book ever written about the subject; it is the bible of building. It was once a standard text. I doubt that most architects read it now, but in its fundamentals it remains for the layperson a useful approach to the analysis of architecture.

A building, wrote Vitruvius, must be considered "with due reference to function, structure, and beauty" (*Utilitas, Firmitas,* and *Venustas* in the original Latin). These are the need, means, and art I have already introduced. Although there are other—and very important—factors to be kept in mind when discussing architecture, as for example economics (a building's budget), this is an exquisite formulation. It is by far the most succinct and at the same time most encompassing definition of architecture ever written, and it will serve as the backbone of my discourse.

Architects think geometrically, and so must we. Envision Vitruvius's definition as an equilateral triangle with one of his factors at

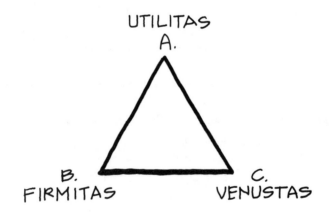

UTILITAS
A.

B.
FIRMITAS

C.
VENUSTAS

ARCHITECTURE

each corner. Each is discrete, yet all combine to shape a larger whole. That larger whole, represented by our equilateral triangle, is the work of architecture. Architecture being an art, and therefore the result of human effort, such a work requires the participation of three types of individuals who personify Vitruvius's factors. Thus *Utilitas*, need, is expressed though a building program created by the client, the owner of the property or his representative. *Firmitas*, the structural and material means of answering the requirements of that program, is the province of the builder. And *Venustas*, the design or artistic arrangement of those systems and materials, is the responsibility of the architect. (An engineer might serve either the builder or the architect but his efforts are absorbed into their work.)

All three activities could be (and have been) performed by the same person, but, especially in the modern world, that is very rare. The poet Robert Browning thought it a distant dreamland indeed "where every man is his own architect." What is more cogent is that, like the three interdependent corners that join to form our equilateral triangle, or the legs of a camera tripod, each of these factors, each of these individuals, depends upon the other two. The trio of concerns forms a unit until the building is complete. Although many a critic and many an architect have neglected the fact, *client, builder,* and *architect* represent respectively *Utilitas, Firmitas,* and *Venustas,* and if the latter constitute the ABC of architecture, the former embody them.

Any building campaign in which these three individuals are not in harmony will prove difficult if not disastrous. Any analysis of architecture that aspires to completeness must recognize the mutual contributions of each. The architect is, however, the pivotal figure. There have been books and exhibitions dedicated to "architecture without architects," but they have merely failed to call a spade a spade, or to credit the designer, whoever he or she was, with the title I find comfortable here. Someone gives form to even vernacular buildings; I choose to call that someone an architect.

Professional or amateur, the architect usually directs the building campaign. The architect interprets the client's program and represents it to the builder. As designer, the architect gives shape to the client's needs and the builder's materials. This is usually expressed through geometrical diagrams, or architectural drawings. There are three basic types of architectural graphics: *plans, sections,* and *elevations.* As it happens, each of these directly relates to each of the three Vitruvian factors. Need, or use, is diagrammed in the floor plans; overall structure (among other things) is depicted in the sections; and the overall design is shown in the elevations.

Plans are horizontal slices through the building at each floor showing the lateral arrangement of rooms. Sections are vertical slices showing upright spatial relationships, the structure, and (in modern buildings) the mechanical systems. They also show the elevations of individual interiors. Elevations are drawings of interior or exterior walls undistorted by the effects of perspective. They show measurable areas and relationships. They are analytical diagrams rather than evocations of intended visual experience.

Supplemental drawings such as full-scale details, diagrams of mechanical equipment, or presentation perspectives enhance the package of architectural graphics, and many are required as part of the contractual process of erecting a complex modern structure, but they are not essential in shaping the basic building. A three-dimensional model costs money and when constructed often acts only as a promotional aid.

Architects in the recent past have usually drawn in pencil or ink on tracing paper or tracing cloth, then made copies for use as "blue line," "black line," or ozalid prints, although increasingly they now generate diagrams by CAD (Computer Assisted Drawing) programs, plot them by machine, and distribute them by printout. However

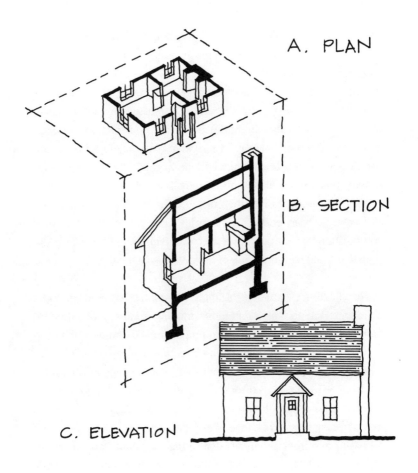

A. PLAN

B. SECTION

C. ELEVATION

ARCHITECTURAL DRAWING

they are produced, they are drawn to scale, usually, in the United States, a quarter-inch to the foot for plans, sections, and elevations, larger to full scale for details.

Multiple sheets of architectural drawings are the rule now in the creation of a building, but there was a time when such graphics were nonexistent, or minimal at best. Few construction drawings for ancient or medieval buildings survive. The drawings for venerable Independence Hall in Philadelphia, begun in the 1730s, consist of two rudimentary plans and an elevation on one small sheet of vellum. This was possible then because the building was designed and erected in a period of universally accepted rules of classical composition and conservative structural technique. It was also designed without regard for any of our present-day energy-driven conveniences.

The difference between the minimal graphics needed for Independence Hall and the voluminous drawings required for a modern building brings up another controlling element that must quickly be recognized in our discussion of architecture: History. While the relationship among the corners of the Vitruvian triangle never varies, the triangle itself moves through time. As it moves, the possibilities of the client's needs, the builder's technologies, and the architect's formal inclinations all change. Before the age of air travel, no client asked for an airplane hangar. Before the Industrial Revolution, no builder erected a steel and plate-glass skyscraper. Before the Middle Ages, no architect designed a Gothic cathedral. Architecture is a discipline located at the intersection of social, technological, and artistic history.

The Vitruvian triangle moving through time creates architecture and its history. It might even be said that architecture and history are inseparable; that architecture *is* history. A building exists as a crystallization of a given moment of society, technology, and art. It is an event in the ongoing evolution of architecture, and it will

probably show the accumulated results of much that has gone before. It is therefore essential that the client, the builder, the architect, and the architectural critic all have at least a basic understanding of architectural history.

Client, builder, and architect represent constituencies larger than
themselves, and those constituencies are shaped by time. The client
stands in for society as a whole or in its parts. A priest ordering a
chapel does so for his congregation, and that congregation is the

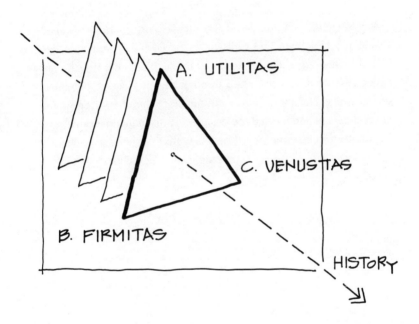

VITRUVIAN TRIANGLE MOVING
THROUGH TIME

creation of historical forces. The builder embodies the current state of technology. The Roman engineer who threw up the great vaults of the Baths of Caracalla used structural potential unknown to (or at least unused by) the earlier Greeks. The architect stands in for the artistic community as a whole. Although much of the rhetoric around such "form givers" as the twentieth-century American architect Frank Lloyd Wright denies the fact, at any given time it would be impossible for a successful designer to break away from the social needs, technological possibilities, or stylistic expectations of his age.

Architecture, then, stands at the intersection of societal need, available technology, and artistic theory. Each of these is represented by the client, the builder, and the architect, but it is the architect who answers the need through the production of plans, sections, and elevations that make apparent the client's program, the builder's materials, and the designer's artistic inclinations.

Architecture is, or at least it begins with, the enclosure of habitable space. We will refine and extend that definition as we proceed.

A IS FOR *UTILITAS*

Architecture begins with *Utilitas*, with need. The need a building is meant to serve, its function, is expressed by society through the client. The modern architect gives form to that need in a plan and other graphics, and the builder makes material the forms evoked by function.

That building must be rare that was erected only to keep heat in and rain off; most buildings have a much more complex generation. Large historical forces concentrate upon the client, and this is true whether the client is a public body or a private individual. Because statistics on crime show an upsurge, a county in the person of its sheriff orders a new prison. Because up-to-date methods of teaching require computerized classrooms, a city through a building committee appointed by the school board orders new schools, or the remodeling of existing ones. "White flight" from the cities of the United States creates middle-class demands for suburban homes with two- or even three-car garages. The technological revolution has made it financially possible for a software wizard to afford a villa in the Bahamas as well as one on the Riviera. With private heliports, please. To study architecture means to study the society that ordered it.

An individual or a group in society identifies a need that can be answered only by building. Alone or in consultation with a planning specialist, the architect, or both, the client draws up an oral or written statement of all that is needed or wanted. This document is the *building program*. It details the necessary and the desirable features that must be present in the building as well as specifies the site, states the budget, and clarifies other limiting factors. The program defines the type of building to be erected—school, fire station, church, field house—as well as the areas that will compose the whole and their square footage. A church usually requires a narthex, nave with transepts, chancel, vestry, and so on; a school needs classrooms, auditorium, gymnasium, offices, restrooms, and the corridors and (perhaps) stairs to join them. The building program lists each of these required areas in turn.

But the program can do more than that. The client often goes beyond the listing of designated areas and square footage to specify what the building should represent. As I shall discuss later, architecture is a form of communication, buildings send messages, and many a client will try to articulate and have the architect express what that message might be. A chief executive officer contemplating the erection of his company's headquarters might want not merely a lot of usable office space but also a corporate emblem. An image of the spiky Transamerica Tower in San Francisco identifies the company's trucks all across the country. A rabbi building a new synagogue will not want it to look like a supermarket, or a church or a mosque. An airline executive might want a new terminal to express the soaring efficiency of flight. That must have been Eero Saarinen's intent, and we assume his client's, when he designed the arcing roofs of the TWA Terminal at JFK Airport in New York. These concepts go beyond the concrete. They are often to be found in the building program, and they therefore, with the listing of physical needs, become part of the client's charge to the designing architect. The more articulate the program, the more precise the charge, the better and the more economically, presumably, the building will achieve and hence serve its intended use.

The history of the design of the complex recently created for the J. Paul Getty Trust in Los Angeles dramatically illustrates the need for a well-drafted building program. The process unnecessarily consumed a great deal of time and huge expense not only because of the many parts of the Trust competing for pieces of the budget, but because of "the center's still inchoate sense of its own identity and

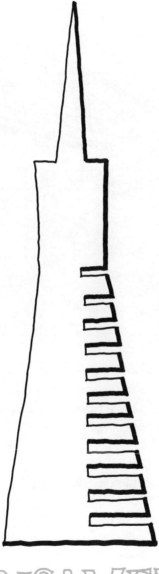

TRANSAMERICA

TWA AT JFK

purpose" during the writing of the program for the architect Richard
Meier, according to the May 1996 issue of *ARTnews*. Initial and
subsequent designs had to be scrapped because of the confusion,
and design revisions continued during construction. Builders call
such late revisions "change orders"; they are expensive necessities
in rescuing a flawed project. The deep-pocketed Getty Trust could
afford to pay for such confusion in its building program; the average
client usually cannot.

Think of the client's program as the foundation or footings of an
actual building. If those footings are weak, everything above will be
ill-founded, and that can mean extensive and expensive repairs or
perhaps even total collapse. Sturdy foundations and a solid program are both essential as the bases of good building.

Architecture begins as idea, passes through literature, and ends as form. The literature, the building program, represents wishful thinking; the building, its fulfillment. It is the task of the architect to turn the program into its three-dimensional equivalent. The process thus becomes a geometrical one. The architect translates words into shapes on paper or in cyberspace, first as a two-dimensional analytical diagram, then as a measured plan, next as sections and elevations prescribing three-dimensional form, and eventually as drawings of details. Thereafter the builder, usually under the supervision of the architect, turns these images into three-dimensional reality.

The plan is the developed diagram of function. Room shapes and sizes, lateral room arrangements, and connections, all assume their proper roles in the building as the architect studies and restudies them. The twentieth-century Philadelphia architect Louis I. Kahn, following the rational planning principles of the French educational system, divided interiors into served and servant spaces. In a school, the served or *primary* spaces—primary because the building is built above all to contain them—are the classrooms, auditorium, and gym; the servant or *secondary* spaces are the corridors and restrooms and offices that permit convenient access to and use of the classrooms. The architect begins a design by sorting out primary and secondary spaces and arranging them into a useful pattern.

The arrangement of the spaces will depend on the building type, the period in history, and other special factors, but there are in general only two ways the individual spaces in a plan can be gathered into a whole: either by *addition* or *division*. (In some instances the two may join in a single building, but I am concerned here with generalizations, not exceptions.) The additive plan is a series of discrete rooms that often results in an irregular perimeter; the divisive plan is created by subdividing a large and usually simple shape—a square or rectangle, say—into smaller rooms. An example of addi-

tive composition in recent architecture is Louis Kahn's design for
the Richards Medical Research Laboratory at the University of
Pennsylvania. There, each unit in the disjointed plan of the building
is clearly articulated. The Gothic cathedral, composed of individual
bays in plan, provides a historical example. Ludwig Mies van der
Rohe's Crown Hall at the Illinois Institute of Technology in Chicago
is an example of divisive planning. The perimeter is a rectangle;
those few separate rooms identifiable within the all-encompassing
interior are set off by subdivision within the rectangular external
wall. The plans of most baroque churches are also articulated by
division.

Since, as the twentieth-century Franco-Swiss architect Le Corbusier said, "Le plan est la générateur," a building's plan or "footprint" dictates the shape and arrangement of everything above it.
The additive plan will usually generate a complex three-dimensional form; the divisive plan will commonly result in something
like a parallelepiped. Kahn's Richards Laboratory and Mies's Crown
Hall exemplify the point. But I seem to be getting ahead of my discourse.

Whether articulated by addition or subdivision, the parts of a
plan will be arranged either *symmetrically* or *asymmetrically*.
Whether an architect chooses one planning pattern or the other will
depend on many determinants, including the building program, the
historical period, the inclination of the client or of the designer, the
budget, the site, and so on. The additive plan frequently assumes an
asymmetrical arrangement, as, again, does Kahn's building at the
University of Pennsylvania, and the divisive plan often results in
symmetrical balance, as does Mies's building at the Illinois Institute
of Technology.

The arrangement of rooms in one half of a symmetrical plan will
be the mirror image of that in the other; an axis separates the two
sides. This method comes into the planning process from an exter-

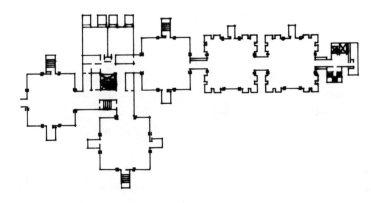

RICHARDS LABORATORY

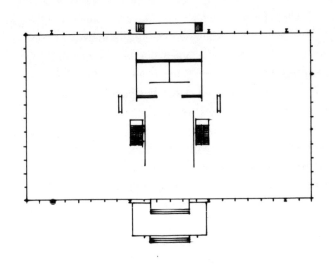

CROWN HALL

nal, a theoretical position. That theory, which in the Western tradition descends from antiquity as interpreted by the Italian Renaissance and shapes the architecture of Michelangelo, for example, or many of Palladio's villas, dictates that the lateral symmetry of the human body ought to be reflected in buildings for human use. An asymmetrical plan, on the other hand, apparently responds directly to the building program. It seems to develop "organically" from the program without regard to theory.

The additive, asymmetrical plan appears to be more flexible than the divisive, symmetrical one. The rule of symmetry precedes any consideration of use. Bilateral duplication is required whether needed or not. The theoretical urge toward symmetry can be an overpowering one, muscling aside any considerations of program, budget, or site. The additive plan can, however, bulge, twist, angle, stretch, or cluster as necessary, without regard to axes, in apparent response to the client's needs. In fact, the organization of asymmetrical plans can be as arbitrary as balanced ones. In practice, structural requirements can often dictate adjustments in either case.

The use of the symmetrical plan, one composed along a main axis or main and secondary axes, is common to some periods or modes of design, such as the classical or neoclassical for example, while unbalanced planning is common to others, such as the High Victorian style. For all its abstractness the plan is such a direct expression of the program that the trained historian can often date and place a building merely from its "footprint." Even in structures of generally similar purpose (for example, houses of religious worship), a work of one era will not look like that of another (unless it is erected in a period in which historical forms are revived, and even then a sharp eye may discern differences) any more than the religion of one region or period will resemble that of another. The plan of the first-century Pantheon in Rome could not be confused with that of a medieval cathedral like Notre Dame at Chartres or that of the Great Mosque in Damascus. Designers created one to house pagan rites (although it was later adapted for Christian use), the second to express Christian worship, and the third to facilitate Islamic prayer. Each was uniquely possible as a diagram of the religious practices only within its own time, place, and people. By the same token, the plan of a Florentine palace of the quattrocento, although it diagrams domestic use, will never be mistaken for that of a middle-class suburban house in, say, Hinsdale, Illinois.

The changing needs of society as it passes through history generate different building programs resulting in different building types. In the Renaissance, architecture embodied aristocratic power, and architectural variety was limited by the needs and wants of the church and state. Cathedrals, chapels, convents, palaces, castles, an occasional hospital: these and a few other types dominated the roster of architectural chores. With the rise of pluralistic, democratic, industrial societies in the nineteenth century, and the parallel revolutions in communications, transportation, technology, and so on, building types began to proliferate. The public library, the railroad station, the air terminal, the concert hall, the car park, the skyscraper: all arose from new building programs generated by new societal needs requiring new planning skills. These new programs joined the older types of the church, chapel, or house. Variety has become so bewildering, and society's needs so complex, that some planners now specialize in one or two building types—hospitals, for example, or schools, or sports complexes.

Variety in architecture is generated not only by the changing needs of evolving societies (reflected in changing building programs and therefore changing plans), but by changes in technological potential as well. What may be structurally possible in one period may be impossible in another. And since the structural system is reflected in the plan, or rather the plan gives rise to the structural armature of a building (remember Le Corbusier), no plan can

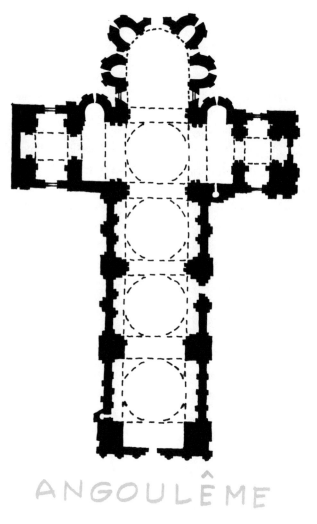

ANGOULÊME

be analyzed without knowledge of the period in which it was drawn, the program it was meant to serve, and the structural system used to achieve the section, or three-dimensional spatial enclosure. The plan of a French Romanesque cathedral, that at Angoulême for example, shows the thick nave walls and massive buttresses that support the heavy domical vaults overhead. The plan of the Gothic

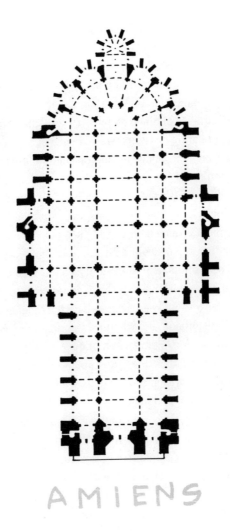

AMIENS

cathedral of Notre Dame at Amiens, on the other hand, shows the footprints of isolated piers and delicate buttresses that absorb the thrust of the sectional groin vaults above. The plan, the diagram of *Utilitas,* cannot be studied without reference to the section and the elevation, to the other corners of the Vitruvian equilateral triangle.

It is sometimes possible to pinpoint the change from one historical era to another by the study of plans spaced only a few years apart. For example, the plan of Burnham and Root's Monadnock Block, an urban commercial building of the mid-1880s in the Chicago Loop, is a thickly outlined rectangular form that reflects the sixteen-story load-bearing masonry walls rising above it. As we shall see, it carries on a prolonged technological tradition that dates back to the beginning of history. The Reliance Building, another commercial skyscraper designed by the same architectural firm and erected a few blocks away just five years later, presents a plan of relatively small piers arranged in a grid. It reflects the presence above of a newly invented, steel-frame structure that would in following decades revolutionize architecture. Again, I would seem to be getting ahead of myself, but in fact it is impossible to consider one Vitruvian factor without keeping an eye on the other two. In my comparison of the Pantheon and Chartres, the difference was seen to be in the program. In my comparison of the Monadnock and the Reliance, the difference is in the structure. In both comparisons there are differences in artistic treatment as well. All the Vitruvian factors are always present and interactive.

No architectural analysis is possible without understanding the designer's diagrammatic response to the building program, but often a copy of the written program does not exist. This is true of the excavated remains of past civilizations, but may also be true of more recent, fully preserved buildings. Since the plan embodies that program, the program can generally be read from the plan. If there is no ready-made plan available, the architectural critic must reverse the process described here. He or she must act as the archaeologist, that is, must try to reconstruct the building program. He or she must measure the building and draw its plan, however roughly. In the absence of a written program, the diagram of function must be re-created on the spot in order to understand, literally, the basic characteristics of the architecture.

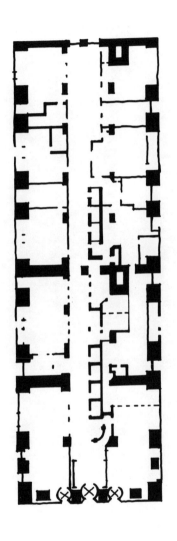
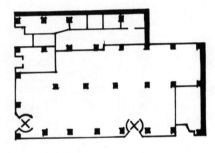

MONADNOCK AND RELIANCE

B IS FOR *FIRMITAS*

If the plan diagrams the lateral relationships among the various items in the building program that have spatial equivalents, the section shows their vertical relationships. Any program that calls for more than one story (that is, one that has requirements that can be met only by going up in the air) will generate sectional drawings. These will show some features, stairhalls for example, running through more than one floor, spaces that are stacked one on top of the other, and so on.

Whether or not the building is to be multistory, when the architect turns to the third dimension in the design process he or she must begin to think about *Firmitas*, or structure. Structure creates the space or spaces that define architecture. Here too there are choices to be made that will depend upon any number of variables beyond the program: budget, availability of materials, the state of technology, the style the building will assume. The requirements of the plan play a role as well, and the designer's choice of structure might modify the diagram of use, just as the choice of style might modify both the plan and the structural system. As I have occasion to observe over and over again, the Vitruvian factors are interdependent. I have not been able to mention *Utilitas* without mentioning *Firmitas*. Although I may discuss them sequentially, the wise architect will begin to think about them all at the beginning of a project. The astute critic or historian of architecture will proceed in the same way.

Older buildings are technically simpler than newer ones, but they all required the engineer's skills. Structural engineering, especially modern structural engineering, is a sophisticated subject. Most architects have on staff or hire as needed people trained to calculate the solutions to complex structural problems. Public safety demands that licensed experts design and check all but the simplest systems. This means that the architect and the architectural critic will probably not understand all the subtle nuances that make up a structural solution, from the calculations of bending moment to those for shear stresses. That does not mean, however, that either the architect or the critic can ignore the structure of a building. Each must be able to grasp some basic engineering principles.

Economics and geography play important roles in the realm of technology. In the contemporary world, in particular in some developing countries, certain materials and "high-tech" systems are not available. Thus, the designer's or builder's options are limited. History, too, plays a leading role in the realm of construction, just as it did in the realm of function. Some structural systems were unavailable in certain periods of the past; some structural materials came into production only with the Industrial Revolution. The age of a building can often be read as accurately from its technology as from its plan. For example, hand-wrought iron nails preceded machine-cut wire nails.

A building's age can also frequently be read from the materials used. The earliest buildings were built of natural materials, or materials crafted from natural products. Stone and timber are basic to traditional architecture, as is concrete, as well as brick and its offspring, tile and terracotta. Stone can be used both structurally and decoratively: granite for posts, slate for roofs. Wood also has both constructional and ornamental applications. Glazing occurs early—the Gothic cathedral is unthinkable without its great stained-glass walls—although the units of glass were small until the Industrial Revolution. Metal, too, had multiple uses: copper for roofs, iron for clamps and ties, lead for the cames holding together the pieces in stained glass; all were used without creating an overall architectural impact.

With the end of the eighteenth century and the beginning of the Industrial Age, new, manufactured materials or old materials capable of new potential transformed architecture. The structural use of cast and wrought iron in large sections revolutionized our capacity for spatial enclosure, and the introduction of steel and reinforced concrete a century later raised that capacity to an even higher level. In the twentieth century plastics further altered the architectural landscape.

New technologies also changed the potential of traditional materials. Traditional wood-frame construction used heavy timbers with mortised and tenoned joints fastened with wooden pegs. Timber in small units, cut by power saws and held together with machine-made nails in balloon-frame construction, changed the look of domestic design in the nineteenth-century United States and also reformed the housing market. Large sheets of rolled and tempered glass called plate glass meant that twentieth-century enclosures could be transparent rather than solid as in earlier buildings.

History, then, produces variables in building materials and structural technology. But just as in the realm of planning there are constants through time—the choices between additive and divisive, between symmetrical and asymmetrical composition—so too in the realm of structure there are constants. As the nineteenth-century critic John Ruskin wrote, "Architecture is the adaptation of form to resist force." The architect's choices of structural form have always been limited. Structural systems are mainly *trabeated*, or *arcuated*, or a combination of the two. The forces to be resisted are also few in number. All structures seek stasis, a statical balance between *tension* and *compression*. The architect, or the structural engineer hired by the architect, no matter when or where he lives, whatever the dictates of the building program, whatever the size of his budget, has freedom of choice only within these limiting gravitational factors.

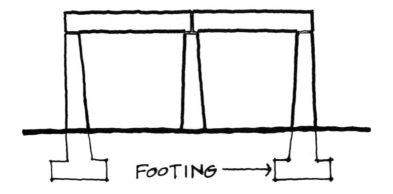

FOOTING ⟶

TRABEATED

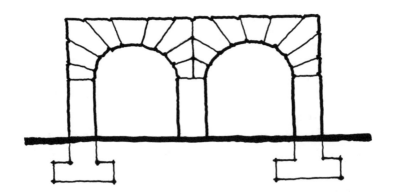

ARCUATED

In structural design, choice of system and choice of material go hand in hand. Some materials better resist tension than compression. Some materials are better adapted for trabeated rather than arcuated construction. Some materials can withstand long exposure to the elements, some cannot. We can now say that architecture is the arrangement of appropriate materials in appropriate structural systems to achieve a useful and—anticipating the next section—perhaps even a beautiful enclosure of space.

Spatial enclosure, although not in the sense of usable space as we might define it, begins in distant time with monuments like Stonehenge on Salisbury Plain in England. There, thick upright stones, or posts, support heavy horizontal stones, or lintels, crossing between them to create slender voids. This primitive post-and-lin-

STONEHENGE

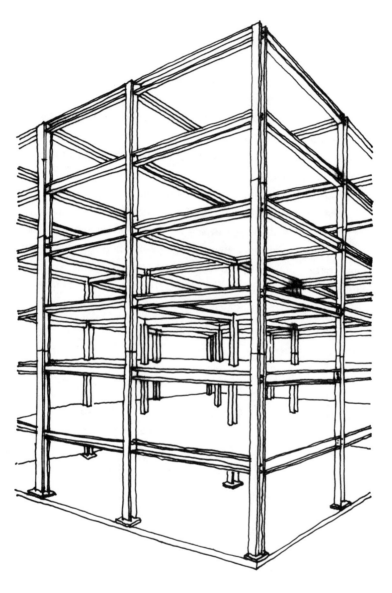

SKYSCRAPER FRAME

tel, or trabeated, structural system is a progenitor of all similar rectangular spatial enclosures, from the wooden Imperial Villa at Katsura in Japan to the steel-frame Empire State Building in Manhattan.

The difference between Stonehenge and the Empire State Building is basically historical rather than statical, in that the posts and lintels of the New York skyscraper are steel not stone, and structural steel is a synthetic product of the nineteenth century. As steel is stronger than stone, the modern structure can be lighter than its ancient ancestor, and the distance between the upright supports can be greater in the younger building. The amount of space enclosed at Stonehenge is limited by the size (length or depth) and the point of fracture of the stones available to span between the posts. Because of its great height, the Empire State Building requires, as we shall see, bracing not present at Stonehenge; nonetheless, Stonehenge, the Empire State Building, and all other buildings erected through history on a trabeated system are members of the same structural family.

The Egyptians and the Greeks introduced many sophisticated visual refinements into the trabeated system used by the builders of Stonehenge, but they did not essentially change it. The classical orders—Doric, Ionic, and Corinthian—are systems shaped by subtle proportions and endowed with a pantheon of meanings, but they are fundamentally arrangements of posts and lintels (or, what amounts to the same, walls and lintels). In the Parthenon the weight of the lintel and all that is above it rests perpendicularly upon the posts, which carry it directly to the ground. The lintel and its supports are at rest; the distance between the supports depends upon the strength of the stone available for the lintel. In general, the use of the trabeated system gives a building a solid, boxy shape, with straight vertical or (occasionally) battered walls or closely spaced upright columns, and a flat or peaked roof.

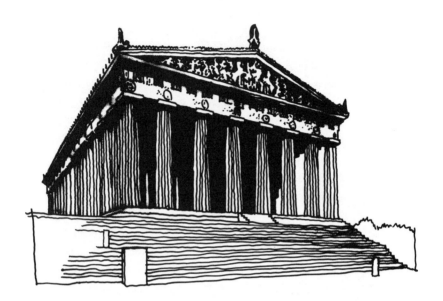

PARTHENON

I need to clarify two points made above. I said that the posts carry the load to the ground. In all but the most primitive structures, that load is in fact carried down through the surface of the ground to the footings. A footing distributes the weight descending through the post just as feet spread the weight of the human body. Its larger surface reduces the pounds per square inch pressing on the soil. In older buildings the footing was frequently made of stone, but reinforced concrete is currently used. Its design will vary with factors such as the amount of the load, conditions of the soil, and so forth. It is an essential albeit invisible component of the structural unit.

Second, I said that the post-and-lintel system generally produced a solid, boxy shape. If we place enough of a load above one end of a beam, or above one of its supporting piers, we can remove the other pier. The result is a beam free at one end, projecting into the void. You can demonstrate this to yourself by holding a pencil at one end with thumb and forefinger. If we move the supporting pier to the center of the beam, if, that is, we balance the beam on a central pier, we will have two free ends pointing into the void. Such a "floating" beam end is called a *cantilever.* A cantilever opens up the trabeated solid.

The use of the cantilever, the length of which depends on the strength of the beam or the amount of counterbalancing weight piled on one end, will create in three dimensions open rather than closed building perimeters. There are structural reasons for using a cantilever, but its choice is most commonly an aesthetic one. In many of his buildings Frank Lloyd Wright exploited the cantilever, as he said, to destroy the box, and thus to open the architectural

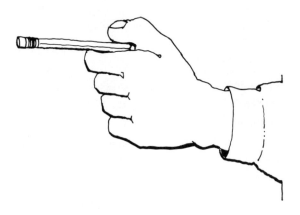

CANTILEVER

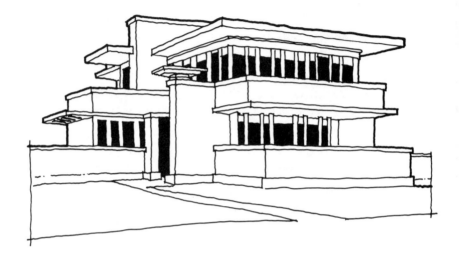

GALE HOUSE

form to its surroundings. His early house for Mrs. Thomas H. Gale in Oak Park, Illinois, is a good example. The cantilever is a most flexible tool within the kit of trabeated structural parts.

In architecture, mass wholly or partially encloses space. At Stonehenge, the Hypostyle Hall of the Great Temple of Ammon at Karnak in Egypt, the Parthenon at Athens, and other early structures, the amount of mass needed to enclose a space was great relative to the amount of space enclosed. These early buildings are heavy and solid. Their builders achieved a minimum of spatial enclosure for the amount of natural materials (baked mud, stone, brick, wood) invested in structure. With the coming of the Industrial Revolution and the manufacture of stronger and relatively lighter synthetic materials (cast or wrought iron, steel, reinforced con-

crete), structural mass began to diminish in relation to enclosed
space. Modern buildings can be lighter—and more spacious—than
ancient ones, even when they incorporate identical structural systems.

Ancient buildings sit heavily upon the earth. Their accumulating
weight spreads visibly outward as it descends. Think of the Egyptian
pyramids, or battered pylons such as those at the Temple of Horus
at Edfu, and, characteristically, the more subtly broadening silhouette of a Greek temple from the ridge at the top of the gable to the
ground at the bottom of the stylobate. The translation of the traditional trabeated structural system into industrial materials meant
that a building could be made to seem to defy gravity, to tiptoe
upon the ground. Plate glass set between thin steel or reinforced
concrete piers at the bottom story of a building, or freestanding

EDFU

piers or *pilotis*, will make it seem almost to float above its site. I have in mind such chestnuts of twentieth-century modernism as Le Corbusier's Villa Savoye at Poissy outside Paris, or Skidmore, Owings & Merrill's Lever House on Park Avenue in New York City.

Architects achieve the effect of lightness by using glass and steel, and by the breadth of the span; as I have said, the span is short for ancient stone works, long for modern steel beams. Stability can be increased by running diagonal or other braces from post to beam, thus reducing the length of the unsupported span. But there is an even more important reason for using diagonal braces in the modern trabeated system.

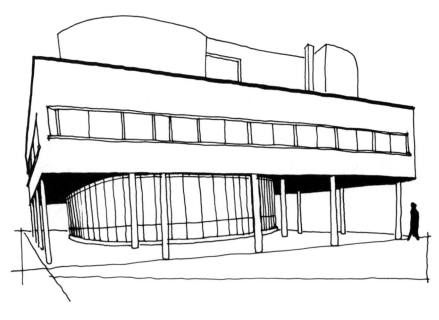

VILLA   SAVOYE

The forces resisted by form are generated by two kinds of loading on a building. There is the *dead load,* or the static weight of the materials themselves, of roofs, walls, floors, and other structural members, and the *live load,* or the dynamic forces on the structure generated by movement of a building's occupants, by winds, by traffic crossing a bridge. The sum of the two is the total of the forces to be resisted by any choice of structure.

The post-and-lintel unit is, as I have said, a stable one, but it is not the sturdiest structural form. As a rectangle, it has the potential of wracking or collapsing under live loads, unlike a triangle which is the most stable of shapes. This is a characteristic of some importance in the design of modern trabeated buildings. Some of them are large, and this is especially so in the case of the urban office building or skyscraper. The structure of such tall buildings not only must withstand pressures from the dead or live loads of its materials and its occupants—pressures that act along its horizontal and vertical members—but must also withstand lateral live loads, that is, external forces generated by wind pressure.

The modern post-and-lintel system, then, often requires wind bracing in the form of triangular members or gussets that prevent the wracking that can occur in the rectangular armature. Such bracing in effect triangulates the rectangle. The diagonal wind brace modifies for new conditions a structural system as old as architecture itself. Architects often conceal such bracing in the finished product so that it plays no role in the visual design. The architects of the Bank of China Tower in Hong Kong, and the architects Skidmore, Owings & Merrill at the John Hancock Building in Chicago, however, exposed for dramatic architectural effect the structures' huge diagonal or X-shaped bracing.

Not all structures in antiquity were trabeated. Through the use of natural materials it was possible to achieve lighter and larger buildings by changing the structural system. The Romans, renowned for

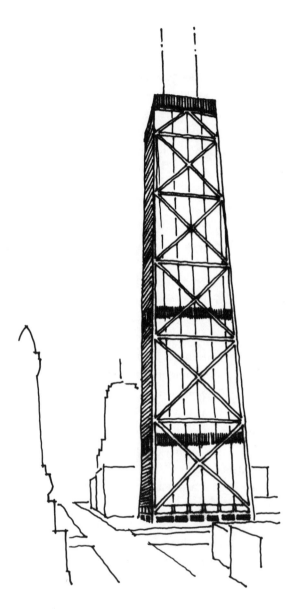

HANCOCK BUILDING

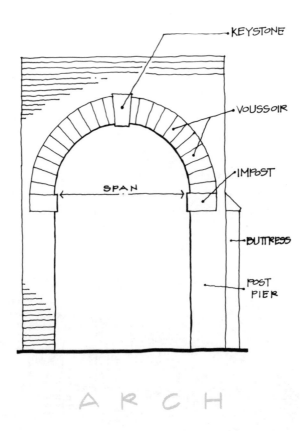

KEYSTONE

VOUSSOIR

IMPOST

SPAN

BUTTRESS

POST
PIER

A R C H

their engineering skills, appropriated the arch, and by extension the vault and the dome, as their basic structural units. The arch shows technological advance over the post and lintel because it avoids the limitations of the one available stone horizontal member by using relatively small stones in combination to achieve relatively large spans. The voussoir, or wedge-shaped block, is the unit of fabrication, and it is easier to man-handle than a large lintel. Placing one voussoir next to another creates a curve rising from the sides of an opening, the piers, to a topmost unit, an often enlarged and ornamented keystone, that locks the system into a unit. During construction, the loose voussoirs are placed on a round form, or centering, until the keystone is dropped into place. The centering can then be removed. The ratio of mass to span, or enclosed space, can be greatly reduced in the arcuated versus the trabeated system.

The arch or a series of arches, an arcade, exists in a straight plane, perhaps most impressively in the second-century Roman aqueduct, the Pont du Gard at Nîmes in the south of France, or in a curved plane, as at the ancient Colosseum in Rome. (The Romans, as they did on the exterior of the Colosseum, often combined the arch with the post and lintel. The latter is decorative, however; the structure itself is arcuated.) Many a monumental interior in the Is-

COLOSSEUM

lamic world depends upon multiple arcades, as in the Great
Mosque at Cordoba.

If the half-circular arch extends into the third dimension by pro-
longation along a horizontal axis perpendicular to its span, it becomes a vault, specifically a barrel vault. If it extends into the third
dimension by rotation around its vertical axis, it becomes a hemi-
spherical dome. Many of the great works of classical Roman architecture were generated by the vault, as in the Baths of Caracalla,
and by the dome, as in the Pantheon. These buildings encompass

CORDOBA

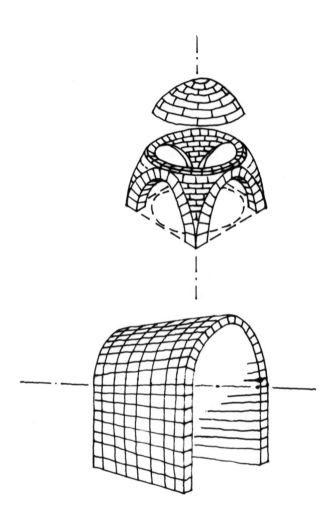

DOME ON PENDENTIVES
AND BARREL VAULT

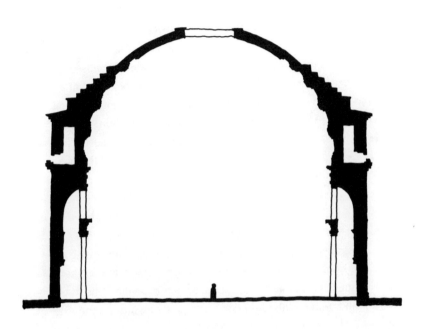

PANTHEON

vast amounts of space unprecedented in the Greek world or earlier. At 142 1/2 feet, the span of the masonry dome of the Pantheon remained unsurpassed until the end of the eighteenth century and the introduction of lighter and stronger iron as a structural material.

I have described the post-and-lintel structural unit as stable, at rest; the weight it supports as flowing perpendicularly into the footings; and buildings erected with that rectangular system as blocky (unless the cantilever is much in evidence). The arch is a curvilinear form that generates diagonal forces that require buttressing, and thus the arcuated building often assumes a rounded or sloping silhouette. A load above an arch must move over and down on an angle in order to reach the lateral piers that take it to the ground. The arch-on-piers structural unit is not of itself stable, because it radiates forces both downward and to the side. The footings will absorb the downward weight, but the lateral energy must be dissipated by one of several means: by the counteraction of other arches, buttresses, or compensating weights piled on the back of the haunches, the curves of the arch between the tops of the piers, or imposts, and the keystone. Occasionally, iron tie-rods were used to prevent the imposts from spreading.

An arch will counter the diagonal thrust of its neighbor, but a series of arches cannot go on forever, so eventually there must be some mass at each end of an arcade to absorb the accumulating energy. This could be a thickened pier. At the Pont du Gard and similar structures, it is the side of the gorge itself that confines the thrust. We are all familiar with buttresses from the flying arcs on the exteriors of Gothic cathedrals. These arcs spread the load generated by the vaults above the nave. The buttresses distribute the overhead weight diagonally, as the transverse section through the nave and side aisles demonstrates, like a person standing with feet planted far apart. A glance at the section or silhouette of the Pantheon will reveal the stepped rings of masonry at the base of the dome that counteract its diagonal thrust.

The dome and the vault predominate in Roman architecture, and in the architecture of some later ages. An extended and richly varied series of architectural forms can be generated by elaborating on these two basic spatial types. If you intersect a barrel vault at ninety degrees with another of the same size, you will get a cruciform in plan whose intersection is covered by a groin vault. If you slice off the top of a dome and place a smaller dome above the horizontal cut, you achieve a dome on pendentives. At its simplest, a pendentive is a spherical triangle transforming a square plan into a circular

HAGIA SOPHIA

one. The barrel-vaulted and the domed space can be joined along one or more axes to form a domed basilica or other large room. And from this basic ecclesiastical unit can be generated any number of richer and richer combinations.

The great Byzantine church of Hagia Sophia at Constantinople (now Istanbul) is an early and outstanding example of a dome on pendentives dominating a vast interior. Since ribs carry the weight of the dome, it was possible to open the webs between them at its base. This produces the halo of windows that makes it appear as if the dome is floating, unsupported by anything but faith, above the heads of the congregation. At Hagia Sophia, *Firmitas* and *Venustas* intersect dramatically.

SAINT PETER'S

Later examples of the impressive use of vaulted and domed structural units can be found in the Italian Renaissance, when architects
revived Roman forms and Roman methods. The sixteenth-century
basilica of Saint Peter's in the Vatican is one of the great works of
monumental arcuated stone building. As finally completed, it joins
a vast nave covered with a barrel vault which is penetrated by
lunettes with a broad-domed crossing that is surrounded by
transepts and chancel surmounted by quarter-spherical vaults. In

Saint Peter's the Renaissance created a vaulted architecture worthy of the ancient classical forms that were its models.

Other ages created lighter structures by using vaulted cellular spatial units added together to create, say, the nave of a church or cathedral. It was easier to build these large interiors one unit, or bay, at a time, and it was easier to achieve the vaults themselves by building them of a framework of ribs infilled with webs. French and English Gothic builders generated quadripartite, sexpartite, and other vaulting forms upheld by isolated piers and flying buttresses, taking them to ever more dizzying heights. Higher and higher, lighter and lighter, and more and more pointed they became, until the builders of Beauvais overreached the limit and the vault collapsed.

Pointed arches or vaults are the sine qua non of Gothic architecture. They are more flexible than semi-circular arches, which must span identical distances if their keystones are to rise to the same height. Since a group of pointed arches can span differing distances while maintaining their keys at the same height, they can rise above all sides of rectangular as well as square bays to produce vaults whose crowns are at constant height. These vaulted bays in series compose the Gothic nave. This permits elastic planning, and it also generates soaring lines. Since such vaults can rest on isolated piers of stacked stones, the space they span can be infilled with diaphanous colored glass. The result is a brittle but spatially flexible, lightweight, largely glazed form racing skyward above its cruciform plan to dissipate into multiple towers and spires. This configuration has come to be seen as the most vivid expression of medieval spirituality. The Gothic cathedral is the perfect example of the indispensability and interdependency of the Vitruvian factors in the creation of a work of architecture. My discussion of *Firmitas* has again led me to anticipate my later discussion of *Venustas*.

The semi-circular and the pointed arch are the basic forms, but over space and time a large assortment of other shapes has evolved. These range from the horseshoe of Islam to the ogee of the late Gothic in Europe. Such variations are largely decorative rather than structural, and all more or less follow the static laws of the basic type.

Although the arch is preeminently a lithic structural form, like the post-and-lintel system it has found employment in the industrial world. At the Sunderland Bridge in England the arch constructed in the 1790s used cast-iron members that acted as voussoirs. Its single span stretched 236 feet between masonry abutments, far outdistancing the free space enclosed by the ancient Pantheon. The New River Gorge Bridge in West Virginia is supported by a steel arch spanning 1,700 feet. The most dramatic arcuated structures of the modern world, however, are constructed of reinforced concrete—not iron or steel—but I shall get to them later.

Whether it is trabeated or arcuated, a structure must achieve stasis, an equilibrium between the opposing forces of tension and

SUNDERLAND BRIDGE

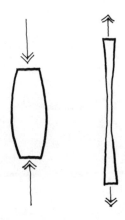

COMPRESSION AND TENSION

compression, or it will not stand up. Tensile forces pull; compressive forces push. If one or the other dominates, the building will tear itself apart. The balance between them in a structural system produces materials at rest that shape usable space. After need is given its due consideration, architecture becomes fundamentally an art of statics.

In the post-and-lintel system the weight of the beam resting on its supports generates compression in each of them. The load pushes directly on the top of each pier while the ground resists that thrust at its base. In the arch the pier and the buttress are also in compression. In either case the pier must be selected (if a natural material such as stone) or designed (if a manufactured material such as steel) so that it will not bend or shorten or collapse under these forces. Its strength is related to its unsupported height. If it is too slender, it will buckle.

The structural calculation for a pier is as simple as the one force it contains. The mechanics of a beam, however, are more complex. When it is loaded, a beam wants to form an upside-down arc. The

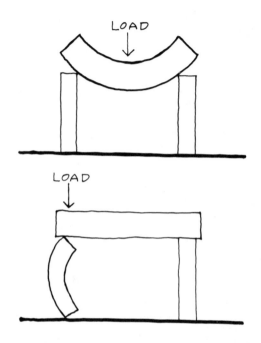

FLEXED BEAM AND
SLENDERNESS OF A COLUMN

top and bottom of the unflexed material that will compose the
beam are parallel and unstressed; but, when that same material
spans between supports, in order to compensate for the stress, the
beam wants to form an arc in which the top and bottom become
concentric segments of a circle. So, the top of the beam must com-
press and the bottom must stretch, or tense. If the beam is not selected or designed so that it is capable of absorbing these opposing
forces, it will rupture. The determinant is the ratio between the

depth of the beam and the length of the span, a ratio that varies, of course, depending on the material used and the load to be applied. The arch has another advantage over the beam in that the arch does not possess such self-destructive forces. Once the keystone is dropped into place, and the proper buttressing established, the arch will stand until it is toppled by external forces.

Some beams show the opposing forces they contain by exposing a tension rod along their bottom dimension. In order to increase its depth and therefore its span, a beam more commonly takes the form of a truss. In a truss the relationship between tension and compression can become complex, and this complexity will often be visibly expressed by the vertical, horizontal, and diagonal pattern of thick compression members and thin tension members. This is especially true when the truss is built of timber compression members and iron or steel tension rods. Wrought iron and steel are strong in tension as well as compression; stone and wood have less tensile value. We can usually read the forces within a truss from visual inspection, unlike those within most beams. Although many trusses are triangular in shape or even have circular segments, if it is properly designed a truss—like a beam—resolves the conflicting forces, applies its load perpendicularly to upright supports, and thus forms part of a trabeated structural system.

Trusses are commonly used today for everything from houses to industrial buildings and bridges. They can be fabricated at the factory and shipped to the building site on flatbed trucks. They, too, had their historical role. The structure of an Early Christian basilica, such as Sant'Apollinare in Classe in Ravenna, differs fundamentally from the Roman public works that preceded it because it is trabeated, not arcuated. The thick counterbalanced vaulted concrete and marble buildings of the Empire gave way in following years to relatively thin brick walls supporting huge wooden beams or, more commonly, trusses. Since the trusses send forces perpendicularly to the ground, there is no need for massive walls or heavy buttresses. Of course, factors other than the technological account for some of the change. The basilicas were planned for a new religion, and they were cheaper to build. It is the change in technology, however, that dominates the difference.

The beam and the arch do not account for all structures. At Eero Saarinen's terminal at Dulles International Airport in Chantilly, Virginia, the roof hangs like a hammock between piers that lean away

SANT'APOLLINARE

from it as they rise. Here the structural system employs neither a traditional beam nor the usual arch, although it does of course recon-
cile opposing tensile and compressive forces. Saarinen's terminal,
like the Golden Gate Bridge in San Francisco and many other buildings and bridges, is a suspension structure. You might think of the
terminal's roof as an upside-down arch hung between the piers that
lean backward, generating compression with which to resist its lateral tension. You might think of the Golden Gate roadway as a
beam hung from the inverted arch above it. It achieves a dramatically long span because it is supported at relatively short intervals
by tensed hangers rising to the inverted arcs. The great piers of the
bridge transfer the tension of the hanging cables and arcs to compression and carry it to the bed beneath or beside the bay. The gap
between these piers far outreaches the diameter of the Pantheon in
Rome or the Sunderland Bridge in England. Modern structural tech-
niques and materials, especially steel cables, make such extraordi-
nary spans possible.

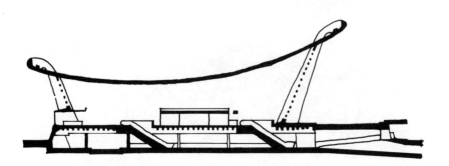

DULLES

The great leaning piers at the terminal in Chantilly are made of reinforced concrete, another modern building material. It combines the old—cement that was known in antiquity—with the new—steel reinforcing bars (or "rebars")—to create a mixed material that can be used to achieve its own architectural shapes. It has been employed in trabeated systems, as in the pre-tensed beams in Kahn's Richards Medical Research facility in Philadelphia. Reinforced concrete beams can be made to counteract their propensity to sag by increasing the tension in the rebars either before or after they are put into place. The hybrid material has also been used in arcuated systems, as in the dramatic bridges of the Swiss engineer Robert Maillart, where valley walls counteract diagonal thrust. It can be warped, folded, creased, platformed, made to fly almost free in breathtaking cantilever construction.

The use of reinforced concrete accounts for some of the most dramatic arched, domed, and vaulted spaces of recent history. These range from the vast, early-twentieth-century Jahrhundertshalle at Breslau, with a span of 213 feet, to Minoru Yamasaki's air terminal at Lambert Field in Saint Louis, where a series of cross

JAHRHUNDERTSHALLE

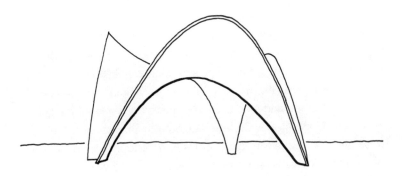

**FELIX CANDELA
CONCRETE SHELL**

vaults covers the concourse. Reinforced concrete can be used in thin sheets that, when curved or creased, become rigid and create dramatic spans and cantilevers. The work of Mexico's Felix Candela exemplifies the point.

After a century of use, however, it is becoming clear that reinforced concrete has some faults as a structural material. The concrete mass and the steel reinforcing bars do not seem to be as compatible as once thought. Where the material has been long exposed to the elements, as in the ordinary highway bridge, severe damage has often occurred. The concrete spalls or flakes off, exposing the rebars to deterioration from the elements. The result may be the detour you are forced to take as you travel by car across the country.

There is one more basic point to be made about structure: it can be revealed or it can be concealed. In nature there are creatures such as turtles who wear their supporting systems, their skeletons, on the outside, and there are others, humans for example, who hide their structure within. Buildings, too, can be exo- or endoskeletal. A great iron-arched train shed or bridge reveals its structure; so does the Eiffel Tower. The roof of Mies van der Rohe's Crown Hall is hung from deep steel beams exposed along the skyline. The suspension systems of the Brooklyn Bridge and similar bridges are there for all to see and marvel at. The trabeated system of the Science Center at Wellesley College is obvious to anyone approaching it. Sometimes exposed structure results from historical accident: the piers of the George Washington Bridge in New York were intended to be covered. Cost prevented their clothing, and we have come to admire their visible steel braces. On the other hand, many of the walls of the average suburban house are load-bearing, and there are probably rafters or trusses under the roof, but we rarely think about them in such terms. What holds up your classroom building, or your dorm, or the library? Structure always impacts upon a building's form; whether it visibly calls attention to itself is a design decision.

Vitruvius's triad, as exquisite as it is, proves inadequate to the modern analysis of architecture in one respect. As an ancient Roman builder, Vitruvius thought of mechanics as structure alone, but the age of energy in which we live has added other technologies to the list, and we must squeeze these, however uncomfortably, into this corner of our triangle. I am referring to plumbing (incoming fresh water; outgoing waste water), to "HVAC" as the professionals initialize it, or the well-tempered interior environment achieved by heating, ventilating, and air conditioning, to "people movers" such as elevators, escalators, and moving walkways, and so on. No usable interior can now be without some or all of these mechanical servants. Like secondary spaces in the plan, they make the primary spaces usable.

Mechanics fit somewhere between need and means, although they can impact on art as well. Heating and air conditioning certainly contribute to, or rather enhance, that fundamental characteristic of architecture that it keep us warm or cool. Space in a plan must be provided for the heater, the air conditioner, the elevator, and so on. The section will reveal ductwork for the distribution of warmed or chilled air, a penthouse for the elevator, hot and cold water risers for the bathroom sinks and showers, waste pipes for the toilets. Any architect who has been misinformed about or has miscalculated the size of the cooling tower or elevator penthouse will know how such essentials will ruin an otherwise well-studied silhouette. Many a modern architect, however, has appropriated such mechanical details into his artistic design. Like an exposed structure, visible pipes and ductwork can give character to a building. The Centre Pompidou in Paris, an art museum, exposes both; so does the Science Center at Wellesley College in Massachusetts.

Construction technologies, building materials, and mechanical devices are the means by which the designer, through the builder, gives three-dimensional expression to the client's programmatic plan. How the architect uses these means, what form the building will assume, what style it will take, are questions to be answered under the third of Vitruvius's rubrics.

C IS FOR *VENUSTAS*

The architect's province is the corner of the Vitruvian triangle labeled *Venustas*. All architects want to plan functionally and build soundly, and all architects want to have a pleasing aesthetic result grow out of this process. These are constants, although they are not always achievable, and sometimes not even compatible. We can now see that even the so-called functionalist architects of the 1920s created buildings not by the literal expression of use or by the direct expression of economical structure, but by the adaptation of patterns of use and systems of structure to classical balance, "dynamic symmetry," or other aesthetic preferences. When the nineteenth-century American architect Louis Sullivan wrote that "form ever follows function, and this is the law," no matter how he has been misinterpreted, he was in fact referring to function as a metaphor of nature, not a rational distribution or even consideration of all the terms of the building program. It might be more accurately said that preferred form more often than not modifies function, and structure too.

By organizing the client's building program in a plan—either by addition or division, either symmetrically or asymmetrically—and by selecting the trabeated structure over the arcuated or suspension system (and therefore probably one material or set of materials over another), the architect has gone a long way toward giving final shape to a building. Those choices often have as much basis in *Venustas* as they do in *Utilitas* or *Firmitas*. Even if plan and structure are closely tied to need and technology, when aesthetics become a consideration, plan and structure may undergo modification. Remember, the Vitruvian factors are interdependent.

Not all buildings look alike, not even buildings erected in the same period and answering the same needs, because there are variables in aesthetics as there are in the other elements governing architectural design. What pleases me does not necessary please you. History is once more the dominant variable, but within any given period economics, location, availability of materials, the needs or the whims of the client, the skills of the builder, the theory of the architect, and more impact on the end product. All these ingredients are mixed in the architect's imagination, and the graphic product pours forth from the end of the drafting pencil or emerges as if by magic on the CAD plotter.

The architect has some control over the plan, the structural system, and the look of a building (that is, its style), but not complete control. The look of a building depends on a host of factors. Marble is out for external walls if the budget cannot provide for it. No tower will enhance a house if the owner will not or cannot pay for it. A skyscraper will not occupy its entire site or rise above twenty-five stories if local zoning laws will not permit it. Metal structural members cannot be exposed in modern buildings because codes require that they be covered with fire-resistant materials. A local committee on "good taste" will reject a design that is too bizarre. Laws governing historic districts seek to maintain the traditional character of a neighborhood, even in new construction. These and many other outside factors enter into and limit the architect's choices at the drafting table or CAD station.

Unlike painting and sculpture, which, although they are usually exhibited in public, are created in private and could remain so forever, architecture is a social art. It exists as a finished product only in public, even when that public is limited, as in a case of a remote mountain cabin or isolated monastic retreat. So the average architect is not as free to "express himself" as is a painter or a sculptor. Society, through the client, orders the architecture it needs or wants. By means of committees on standards of design, historic districts, zoning laws, building permits, and other regulations and regulating bodies and instruments, society tries to ensure that it will get what it can live with.

There are, of course, fantastically wealthy and powerful clients who can manipulate the regulations. And there are "signature" architects: architects who, working with indulgent clients, design largely for themselves, their peers, or the slick magazines, or give society what they think it needs. These are celebrities, creatures of the media who dominate the history of architecture, especially the history of modern architecture: Frank Lloyd Wright, Le Corbusier, and Ludwig Mies van der Rohe among the departed heroes; Robert Venturi, Frank Gehry, and Michael Graves among the living. The bulk of the buildings built, however, have been and are created by less sporting types—some even anonymous—who work within the bounds of social decorum. It is a product of our star-struck educational system that we think only of the "masterpieces" of the "form givers" as worthy of historical or critical discussion. In fact, the Vitruvian triad applies to all building.

Whether a signature architect or not, a designer has in his or her formal "tool kit" a series of concepts with which to work to achieve the final building. These are the elements of architectural design. They begin with decisions about the additive-divisive, symmetrical-asymmetrical, and trabeated-arcuated alternatives of form and structure we have already discussed, and proceed to choices about other dichotomies, such as solid-void (wall-window), planar-plastic (two- or three-dimensional), closed-open, curved-straight, clarity-obscurity, and so on. There are other considerations to be given to design concepts such as scale, proportion, rhythm, and shape. None of these decisions can be made without reference to others, such as color, texture, materials, illumination, focus, and more. And finally, all of these abstractions

will have to become material by shaping, placing, and manipu-
lating walls, roofs, chimneys, ceilings, floors, doors, windows,
wings, porches, stairs, and so forth.

If the architect has used a symmetrical plan to diagram the
client's needs, chances are that the building arising from that plan
will be *formal*. In that case it will probably spread out horizontally
and perpendicular to the axis of approach, show a regular series
of identical bays or windows across the elevation or elevations,
and have its main entry on center in the facade, perhaps enclosed
in a columnar temple front or perhaps emphasized with sculptural
or other ornament. Perhaps the building will even be raised on a
platform and be capped with a pediment or cornice. It might rely
on trabeated or arcuated structure or both, and its interior spaces
and external openings might reflect the choice or the combination. It is often monochromatic.

Such a building might be called classical or neoclassical, especially if the architect enhances it with the vocabulary of architecture that has descended from the Greeks and Romans: the ancient
orders, quoins, cornices, dadoes, and other ornamental features.
Karl Friedrich Schinkel's early nineteenth-century Altes Museum
in Berlin is a textbook example of such a design. If the walls are
enriched with the classical orders, the architect has a choice between planar and plastic forms. In the case of the latter, the
columns can be of various degrees of relief from one-half and
three-quarter engaged to freestanding, as in Schinkel's museum.
The degree of relief, from mural to fully rounded, of any articulation, classical or not, will determine the play of highlight and
shadow on the exterior.

But a building may be thought of as formal or classical even if it
is astylar, or without columnar articulation, if it otherwise meets
the criteria mentioned here. The Palazzo del Lavoro at the Espo-
sizione Universale di 1942 (EUR) in Italy is an arcuated example.
Even the steel and glass buildings of the moderns, who had noth-

ALTES MUSEUM

DESIVOD DLANARIR DNV PIERON
ELENA DDICIS LLI ANOPESCILLIN
DIN RVIVIEDI INSAIVITTNI

PALAZZO DEL LAVORO

ing good to say about the history of architecture, can exhibit classical form. Mies's Crown Hall and other buildings at Illinois Institute of Technology fit into this category. They are broad horizontal blocks divided into a regular series of trabeated bays marked by thin metallic uprights and infilled with either transparent vitreous sheets or precise brick panels, and focused—if only weakly—on an axial doorway.

If the divisive plan frequently materializes as a balanced three-dimensional solid, the additive plan will as frequently generate irregular, or *picturesque*, forms. The designer gives each additional room or cluster of rooms its own three-dimensional shape. He or she achieves in each a discrete enclosure, and the accumulated result is often unbalanced, dynamic, and aggressive. Silhouettes are active, surfaces busy, the interplay of spaces dramatic, and the modeling of masses by sunlight and shadow intense, especially in southern climes. Scale can bounce all over the place, colors and textures vary wildly, shapes begin and end raggedly.

Just as the divisive, formal building lent itself to classical details and associations, so the additive, picturesque building has often lent itself to Gothic accents. The accumulated individual spires intended for Gothic cathedrals, if any one of them had ever achieved its full complement, would have generated a bristling,

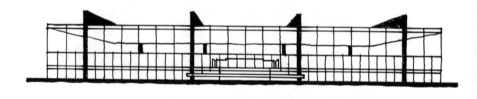

CROWN HALL

activated silhouette. It was the German poet Goethe (following, however, his older countryman Schelling) who so famously described architecture as frozen music, but a High Victorian Gothic building such as the hotel at Saint Pancras Station in London, is, rather, frozen fireworks. Asymmetrically gathering a motley assortment of polychromatic and eclectic pointed forms as it rises from the street, with London's usually dim, occasionally bright sunlight playing like bursts of phosphorescence across richly wrought brick, stone, terracotta, and ironwork surfaces, it finally explodes against the sky in a splintering riot of dormers, towers, and spires. The surfaces of Kahn's Richards Medical Research Building show greater restraint, and overt Gothic forms are absent, but its clustered towers, some with cleft tops, carry the pic-

RICHARDS LABORATORY

turesque aesthetic into the middle of the twentieth century. Frank Gehry's Winton Guest House in Wayzata, Minnesota, brings it into the recent past.

How we read the external form of a building is greatly affected by its site, and by how we approach it. We usually confront a formal building head-on so that its balanced parts are readily apparent; a picturesque one we approach diagonally, so that its irregularities are emphasized.

As important as site—and related to it—is a building's silhouette against the sky. In a formal design this will usually be calm, with a terminating cornice, or, if the roof is visible, with a long horizontal ridge line common to gable or hipped roofs broken at

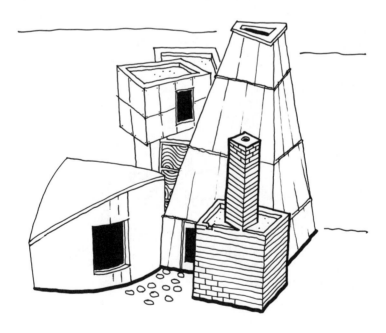

WINTON GUEST HOUSE

regular intervals by discrete dormers and low chimneys. The color of the visible roof, like that of the walls below, will usually be monochromatic. In the picturesque arrangement, as at the Saint Pancras hotel, high, broken roofs are the order. Tall pyramids or cones over lower towers, many irregularly placed dormers, and parti-colored roofing materials all carry the energy of the nether walls into the atmosphere above.

A roof may be flat and therefore not count in the architectural image, or it may be visible. There is a rich variety of roof types available to the designer. The simplest high roof is the gable, with two slopes meeting at a horizontal ridge. A gambrel also has a

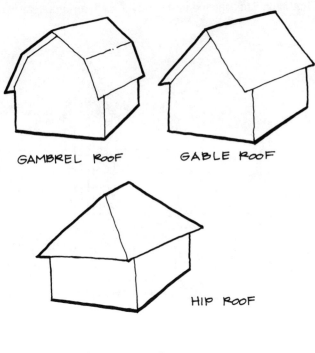

GAMBREL ROOF   GABLE ROOF

HIP ROOF

ROOFS

horizontal ridge but two slopes to each side; it is commonly seen in American barns. A hip roof is one with four slopes rising to the ridge. These basic shapes can be enriched by cross gables or gambrels, by dormers, by towers or turrets, by monitors and skylights. Their visual impact depends not only on shape but on materials as well. Wood shingles, wood shakes, asphalt shingles, tiles, slate, thatch, corrugated sheet metal: all are possible as coverings, and each adds its own character to our reading of the architectural form.

The contrast between symmetry and asymmetry in the arrangement or articulation of three-dimensional form is not restricted to different buildings. It is possible to incorporate such contrast into one building. The nineteenth-century American architect H. H.

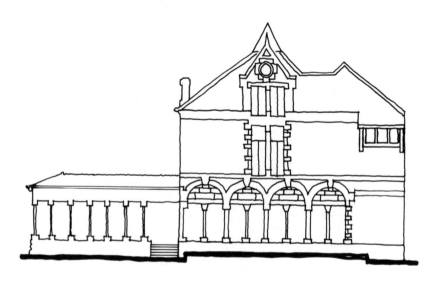

TRINITY PARISH HOUSE

Richardson was a master of such controlled dynamics. In the east elevation of his parish house at Trinity Church in Boston, for example, he stacked arcade, window, and dormer along a central axis, then unbalanced the composition by extending a colonnade to the left and adding to the right a blank bay capped by a window that is hooded by an extension of the roof. We are reminded by such an example that the neat divisions of a primer such as this one cannot account for all the rich possibilities of the real architectural world.

Like additive and divisive planning, or trabeated and arcuated structures, formal and picturesque are constants of *Venustas*, of three-dimensional organization. As my examples have shown, the two recur throughout history and at times appear as alternates within the same era. There may be a period preference for one over the other, but the architect's choice may also depend on other factors. Site or location are important in the decision as well. An urban building might assume one solution; a rural one, another. A rugged site might call for the picturesque; a prime example is the nineteenth-century castle of Ludwig I at mountainous Neuschwanstein in Bavaria. A building in the middle of an urban block will call for one kind of design, while one located on a corner, or freestanding, will suggest another. A location near other buildings might lead the designer to take his cue from them in order to produce a harmonious ambience. Official buildings new and old along the Mall in Washington, D.C., follow this rule. They are formal whether or not they display the trappings of classicism. Of course, the designer might also opt for contrast between his building and its ambience. Le Corbusier's Carpenter Center at Harvard University is a case in point.

The external impact of a building depends not only on the joining of larger forms but on the size, shape, and relationship of its smaller parts, especially of the openings in its walls. That relation-

NEUSCHWANSTEIN

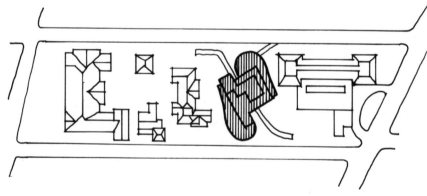

CARPENTER CENTER

ship is not just one of number or dimension; it relates to outline and ornament as well. An opening such as a window may be round, diamond-shaped, square, rectangular, round-arched or pointed, and so on. One of these shapes might be repeated across a wall, as is common in formal buildings, or two or more might be combined into the same facade, as is characteristic of picturesque buildings. It is important to notice, too, whether an opening interrupts a wall or, by means of mullions, panels, or even reflections, continues the exterior surface. That surface is also maintained if doors and windows are set in the outer plane of the wall; recessed doors and windows not only break up the surface but reveal the thickness of the wall. A portal might be broad or narrow, round-headed or pointed; it might contain a single door, double doors, or a bank of doors or be placed symmetrically or asymmetrically within the wall. The doors themselves might be transparent glass or solid wood.

How an opening is framed is of key importance. There may be no frame at all, with the opening merely sliced through the plane of the wall. If a frame exists, it can be minimal, a linear outline of the window, more ornate but still flat, or a shadow-catching plastic composition like an aediculae with projecting columns and a pediment overhead. It can be an architectural frame, like those of Raphael's Palazzo Pandolfini in Florence, or anthropomorphic, like the portal in the guise of a monster's mouth at the Biblioteca Hertziana on the Via Gregoriana in Rome.

To this point I have directed our attention largely to the abstract manipulation of external building blocks, the arrangement and articulation of the mass as a whole and in its parts. To speak of mass is to speak in the concrete terms of materials. The type and characteristics of materials impact upon form and—as we shall see—upon meaning, so the architect of a new building must decide whether he or she wants them to be—or you as a critic must ask

PALAZZO PANDOLFINI

HERTZIANA

whether they are—opaque, translucent, or transparent, smooth or rough, light or dark, natural or manufactured. Is the opaque wall built of stone, wood, brick, or enameled metal panels? Is the stone random or horizontal ashlar, deeply or thinly drafted, rock-faced or dressed, mono- or polychromatic? What kind of stone is used? The range is vast, from expensive marble to common schist, from sturdy granite to crumbling sandstone. For example, marble is a stone, and thinly sawn sheets of marble create translucent panels in the external walls of Skidmore, Owings & Merrill's Beinecke Library at Yale University. Glass might produce transparency, as in Crown Hall, but it might also appear opaque, as in I. M. Pei's John Hancock Building in Boston. Since it also reflects the sky and scudding clouds against which it rises, the Hancock seems almost to vanish. This is an example of transparency of a different sort.

Other questions to ask yourself about a building are: Is the opaque wall made of brick? If so, what size brick? Is it laid in Flemish, English, or common bond? Is it machine-made, handmade, or clinker brick? Is it all the same color or laid up in different colors to create patterns? Is it glazed or matte? Or is the opaque wall constructed of wood? Is it of clapboards, shingles, or plywood panels? Is it painted or stained? What color or colors? If it is of clapboards or shingles, how much has been allowed "to weather"? That is, are they broadly or narrowly exposed to the elements? Or is the opaque wall composed of enameled metal panels? What size, texture, finish, color? How a wall receives external light depends significantly on the material of which it is composed. And light, as we shall see, is a fundamental element of architecture.

The size of these material units, of stones or bricks, the weather dimension of shingles or clapboards, like the size, shape, and interior subdivisions of doors and windows, the magnitude of anthropomorphic sculpture, the height of the risers in stairs and of railings, all create a relationship among themselves. This is called scale. The scale of a building characterizes the design as a whole. There is also a relationship established between these parts, the building as a whole, and you and me that is also called scale. A building is said to be "out of scale" if one part seems to have drifted over from a larger, or smaller, building. It is also said to be out of scale if we feel dwarfed by it or otherwise unrelated to it; in sum, a building is in scale if we feel comfortable using it. Scale is relative, not absolute like size, and it is a factor in the design to which the architect—and critic—must be particularly sensitive.

One way to attempt to achieve human scale in a building is to use a module, a basic dimensional unit that may or may not relate

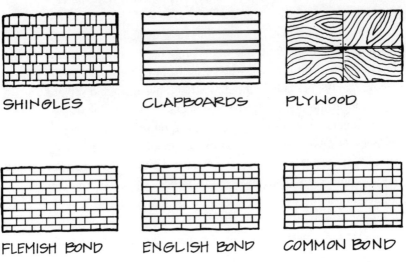

SHINGLES   CLAPBOARDS   PLYWOOD

FLEMISH BOND   ENGLISH BOND   COMMON BOND

WOOD AND BRICK PATTERNS

to the human body. Traditionally, dimensions themselves were expressed in terms of a human unit like the American foot or the Italian *piede*, although these were not always a standard length until the modern era. There have been hordes of modular systems proposed over the course of history. Some, like that of the Greeks, were rational systems based upon a unit, like the diameter of a column, to which all other dimensions related. Since the ancient column was a metaphor for the human body, this was a module that related to the building's users. Some systems were based on the "Golden Section," the irrational relationship between the side of a square and its diagonal. Satisfying proportions of a pedestal or a window opening could be generated using this ratio. A few systems also merged into mystical number symbolism. Le Corbusier proposed his own system based on the human body. The application of most of these systems, even by their inventors, has often been haphazard. There is many a slip between theory and practice.

Size, scale, and materials are intimately related. A brick wall has a different effect from one of concrete block. Its scale is dramatically changed if it is covered with paint or stucco. A bewildering number of choices about materials have been and still are available to the architect. The architect's decisions will, as always, depend on availability, budget, and other practical considerations, but they will also hinge on design factors as well. Scale is one factor; light is another, or rather, how the building reacts to light. Should the building be open or closed? Light passes through an open or transparent building. An opaque building with richly sculpted external walls—whether its modeling comes from the texture of the materials, the use of projecting classical or Gothic or Islamic decoration, or the presence of sculptural accents—will seem to be shaped by light and shade. These will model a solid enriched by chiaroscuro. Light will reflect off a glazed building, leaving an image of its surroundings, although often a distorted one, on its smooth face; by thus merging the building with its environment, light seems to reduce the building's presence within it. As we have seen, Boston's John Hancock Building is a good example of this design technique.

Light acting on shape and materials creates the image we call the exterior of a building, whether that image is seen via direct or diffused sunlight, moonlight, or light from within a building that reaches the midnight voyeur through windows and doors. How openings are placed in the walls will affect the pattern of illumination we see at night on the exterior, and hence our reading of the architectural form, but it will also affect the quality of natural illumination during the day in the interior. We have said that architecture begins with the need for interior space. As Emily Dickinson expressed it more poetically, "The Outer—from the Inner / Derives its Magnitude." We can now add that architectural aesthetics are measured by the quality of interior space. Paraphrasing Frank Lloyd Wright paraphrasing ancient Chinese philosophy, the essence of a building is the space within. The quality of that space will depend on its relationship to adjacent spaces, its three-dimensional shape, the materials used to create that shape, and its illumination.

The additive plan usually results in a series of enclosed rooms; the divisive plan is generally more open. An enclosed space has one effect. If it is opened laterally, vertically, or diagonally into another space or other spaces through doors, windows, screens, stairs, galleries, or whatever, it will have a very different impact. Spatial manipulation is the essence of architectural design, whether that manipulation is for reasons of need, structure, or design.

The length, width, and height of a room are other primary elements in establishing its quality as a space. Floors and walls are

STO. SPIRITO

usually flat (although there can be changes in levels below and
niches and other recesses to the side), but the ceiling can be flat,
beamed, trussed, suspended, vaulted, or domed. Each choice of
structure above will create its own characteristic space below.
There is even great variety within each category. We have discussed the Byzantine arcuated structural and spatial units. A barrel-vaulted rectangular bay is different from a domed square; a

S. GIORGIO MAGGIORE

cruciform bay topped by a groin vault varies in its psychological impact from one topped by a dome on pendentives. Although both are Latin crosses in plan and classical in style, there is a great difference between the interior of Brunelleschi's fifteenth-century Sto. Spirito in Florence and that of Palladio's sixteenth-century S. Giorgio Maggiore in Venice, not the least because the earlier nave is flat-ceilinged and the later is barrel-vaulted.

Where and how natural light enters during the day, and the kind, intensity, and placement of artificial illumination at night, will especially characterize a space. These are all the results of the architect's decisions. Daytime illumination varies according to the size, shape, placement, and number of windows. Is the lighting direct or indirect? The interior of Mies van der Rohe's glass-walled Farnsworth House in Plano, Illinois, is dramatically different from the interior of the Asam brothers' eighteenth-century church of Saint John Nepomuk in Munich. The interior of Rome's Pantheon, naturally lighted by a circular opening or oculus at the apex of the dome, again differs. The Farnsworth is intensely flooded with directed sunlight, while the Pantheon is gently suffused with an even glow. The mysterious interior of the Rococo church in Munich, on the other hand, is barely kissed by indirect light. Differing uses of artificial illumination, through candles, lamps, incandescent bulbs, or fluorescent tubes, will have the same fluctuating results.

Space is characterized by the amount as well as the kind of light within it. Modern glass walls and fluorescent lighting drain the vitality of interior space by bleeding it of shadowed form. Candlelight and older incandescent lighting give character to a space by suffusing it with dusk. Stained glass enhances an ecclesiastical interior because it colorizes the atmosphere. A space derives its quality from the combination of its shape, materials, and lighting.

Color, too, plays a role here. The architect can choose the palette of a building either by the color of finish materials or by the application of wallpaper or paint. Monochromy, polychromy, hue, intensity, saturation, distribution: all these and more impact on the quality of a space as they do on the character of exterior walls. The combination of color and texture, highlight and shadow, solid and void must all be considered by architect and critic alike.

The architect shapes space by enclosing it with structure and materials, then characterizes it by the way he or she manipulates light and color. Sound, too, can enhance space, as anyone knows who has heard the organ fill the colorful interior of H. H. Richardson's Trinity Church on Copley Square in Boston. (The illusive qualities of light and sound in architecture make it impossible to understand a building only through photographs, or even a model. The encompassing characteristic of architectural space must be experienced in situ.) All this is part of the designer's transformation of need, the building program, into art, the aesthetic construct. But architecture can go beyond speechless beauty; it can communicate meaning like any other language.

ARCHITECTURE
AS COMMUNICATION

Architecture is a form of language, of communication. It speaks. It can convey through its design its place in society, its content.

The Philadelphia architect Robert Venturi and those in his circle have divided buildings into "ducks" and "decorated sheds" and have pointed out that each group exhibits meaning in a different way. A duck is architecture modeled by association, a building whose shape suggests its content in the most direct way. It is a clam shack in the shape of a clambox, a roadside restaurant in the shape of a duck or a hot dog, the Brown Derby sculpted as a hat, and so on. Such buildings are visual puns, and the pun has been called the lowest form of humor. This is speaking architecture of

DUCK AND DECORATED SHED

an elementary sort, although for many it represents American popular culture at its most characteristic.

A decorated shed on the other hand is a basic building, walls and a roof, that becomes architecture—or at least conveys a message—by means of what is placed in front of or hung onto it (signs, ornament, and so on). The false-fronted buildings of the towns in movies set in the old West are decorated sheds. They too occupy the bottom of the architectural language arts.

Architecture, especially older architecture, conveys deeper, or broader, or more cogent meaning through metaphor. As we have seen, Vitruvius likened the sturdy Tuscan or Doric columns to male figures, the more slender Ionic to the figure of a maiden, and so on. Thus a temple or monument to a male god or a male hero ought properly to be of Tuscan or Doric style if it is to be erected in a classical style according to time-honored usage. Think of the Lincoln Memorial in Washington, D.C. There is an appropriate form for the message to be sent.

LINCOLN MEMORIAL

Buildings, like other forms of communication, take on or deepen their meaning through quotation. Just as allusions to Shakespeare or the Bible may reverberate through a novel, a poem, or an essay, giving it a depth not otherwise attainable, so quotations from celebrated past architectural monuments or eras can enhance our reading of a building by assuming something of their aura. Such quotations work by authority and/or by association. When Thomas Jefferson designed the Virginia State House in the 1780s, he based its external form on that of the ancient Roman Maison Carrée at Nîmes in the south of France. He did so because he and others of his age thought of that model as exhibiting architectural perfection; they saw the State House as transferring by authority and association that image of perfection to the government of the new state and nation.

However, not all buildings are classical or neoclassical in style. Architecture is more broadly communicative by association, by the appropriation of the accumulated meanings that have adhered to various styles throughout history. By association with particular uses in the past, specific architectural forms have come to embody meaning just as words convey meaning. The appropriate form, like the appropriate word, is necessary if the architect is to get his or her message across. The architect must know history if he or she wishes to speak clearly through buildings. The critic must know history if he or she wants to understand what is being communicated.

This volume is a primer, not a history of architecture; I can here merely recall some salient aspects of the subject. Western architectural history has been written until recently as a kind of Biblical succession of periods exhibiting characteristic forms or styles. Egyptian style begot Greek begot Roman begot Early Christian begot Romanesque begot Gothic. The Renaissance leapfrogged back over what it called the Middle, or "Dark," Ages to take up where the Romans left off, then begot the baroque and rococo. Neoclassicism superseded the Roman with revived Greek forms. The nineteenth century saw a revolution in industrial materials and technology and an eclectic reiteration of all past styles, including what the Eurocentric view called the "nonhistoric" ones. These were the building forms of India, China, Japan, Islam, and so on. One group of twentieth-century architects rejected the historical past, or said it did; other groups embraced it either for the purposes of serious looting or ironical distortion.

Professors taught architectural history as a succession of recognizable "period" or "area" styles in which each of the categories above displayed characteristic forms. To mention a few: Egyptian architecture used heavy lotus columns, massive battered walls, and pyramidal forms. The Greeks built marble temples with low-pitched gables, peripteral colonnades of Doric, Ionic, or Corinthian orders, and small interiors. Rome appropriated the arch and the vault and wedded them to a decorative use of the Greek (and other) orders to build the great public monuments of the Empire with vast interior spaces. The Early Christian church, as we have seen, was thin-walled, trussed, and meant for collective worship by hordes of converts gathered into vast, mosaic-lined basilicas. The Romanesque, as its name implies, revived the vaulted architecture of the Roman Empire but adapted it to the liturgical rites of the Christians and the primitive decorative inclinations of the Goths.

The Gothic style incorporated the pointed arch, vast areas of stained glass, and the soaring proportions made possible by skeletal pier and pointed rib-vault construction. The Renaissance, as advertised, reverted to the forms of classical antiquity but adapted them to Christian humanism. The baroque and rococo twisted the old Roman orders and molded interlocking, more complex geometric shapes that created breathtakingly fluid interiors and richly billowing exteriors. Neoclassicism revived chaste Roman forms and introduced revived Greek ones.

The Industrial Revolution meant both a departure from traditional technologies and a bewildering eclecticism of revived historical forms. During that century the West became aware of the "exotic" styles of the Near and Far East, Africa, and Oceania: the horseshoe arch of Islam, the splayed eaves of Chinese roofs. Finally, some architects in the twentieth century carried on the love affair with history, while others sought a complete break with the past, theoretically elevated originality to the winner's podium, worshipped structure as architecture, and then returned to history either ignorant of its deepest possibilities as a forceful language or ready to subvert history in an iconoclastic attempt to regenerate architecture.

IMPERIAL PALACE
BEIJING

These historical eras and geographical areas were associated with certain societies, so their architectures came to seem appropriate for the building types associated with these societies and, through that process of association, with certain immutable meanings. A client ordering a church for a Christian congregation might expect it to be Gothic, for Gothic forms sprang from the Age of Faith and embodied Christian worship. A park commission paying for a recreational building would happily see it rise in Islamic or Chinese style, for these were considered "nonhistoric" (therefore not serious) and appropriate as backdrops for life's lighter moments. By association with ancient Roman public life, classical forms reeked of government or finance. By their association with the Egyptians' search for immortality, lotus columns and battered walls were applied to cemetery gates and other funereal forms: a nineteenth-century Egyptian Revival gateway (complete with biblical inscription!) fronts Mount Auburn Cemetery in Cambridge, Massachusetts.

In the last two centuries antique and medieval forms have constituted the most common vocabulary of architectural language. Classical forms have evolved an aura of majesty, decorum, even civic virtue. They have generated in the past a sense of longevity, stability, rectitude, even stable power (or contrarily, as in the case of ancient Rome, a cautionary tale of a fallen empire). Classicism stands at the very core of our conception of the federal government at Washington, D.C. What other architectural style could embody the United States Supreme Court? What other than the virile Doric columns of the Lincoln Memorial would form a better, more telling, backdrop to civil rights marches or memorial gatherings? Architects designing such buildings—buildings whose classical parts adhere to the flexible yet guiding principles of the style in the same way a citizen of the democracy might find flexibility yet guidance in her laws—practiced a kind of creative

scholarship. The buildings rose imaginatively out of the accumulated meanings embedded in the inherited forms of the past.

Classicism, like the English language, is precise but flexible. It
can suggest commercial probity, as we see in the classical architecture of bank buildings and, above all, in the New York Stock
Exchange. It can radiate culture, as in the neoclassical art museum in Philadelphia and many another city. In the early nineteenth century the Greek temple form pledged allegiance to the
democratic principles that America traced back to ancient
Athens. Postmodern architects such as Michael Graves or the late
Charles Moore have violated the style's decorum, its nicely
arranged and proportioned parts, in an ironical or mocking edito-
rial on declining cultural standards or their perplexed relationship
to history.

Classicism, as I have said, lends itself to the formal development of the building program. Unless its axes extend out into a
formal garden, it is a style that usually stands aloof from, if it does
not actually dominate, nature. The Gothic, on the other hand, is
not traditionally associated only with the Christian religion; its
meaning has been flexible. Its tall, overarching linear forms were
thought to have been originally inspired by the forest interior, its
nave piers spreading upward and outward in emulation of rows of
trees overbranching a wooded pathway. Gothic seemed appropriate for the "picturesque," a label quickly applied to informal landscape design in England, and it was adopted in nineteenth-
century England and America for use in rustic, usually irregular
cottages and country villas, especially in America, following the
leadership of the architect A. J. Davis and the landscapist and the-
oretician A. J. Downing.

Buildings radiate meaning through the language of form,
through style. If your new local library looks like a cathedral, it
may be because the architect used pointed arches for its open-

ings. (If your new library is a remodeling of a former cathedral, there is reason for that, but here we are not discussing adaptive reuse.) The reason the pointed arch looks wrong is that it is an older form appropriated during the Catholic ages and historically associated with ecclesiastical architecture. The pointed arch is associated with Christian architecture, so a Gothic synagogue would be as confusing as a garbled e-mail message. (There have been Egyptian-style synagogues, which seems contradictory, but when nineteenth-century American synagogues were designed, there were no easily identified Jewish architectural forms, and Egyptian ones were at least associated with the eastern Mediterranean.) The use of the pointed or Gothic arch in a library or a synagogue is really a misquotation. Like the appearance of the wrong word in a sentence, it generates confusion.

TOWER COURT

On the campus of Wellesley College in Massachusetts are two buildings that clearly state through their forms their places in the academic life of the school. One is Tower Court, a dormitory erected in 1915. It is a steel-frame building covered with brick and cast stone exterior walls wrought with the historical attributes of both an English collegiate hall and an Elizabethan country house. These are legible historical metaphors. We read this building as belonging to a college that—when the building was designed—thought of itself as a descendant of the great medieval universities of England, and we see it clearly as a residential enclave. Since its modern structural system is well hidden beneath a historical costume, it radiates academic tradition and domestic comfort. The Science Center built during the 1970s, on the other hand, is an exoskeletal or exposed reinforced-concrete frame and

SCIENCE CENTER

plate-glass building that glories in its references to the present rather than the past. It flaunts rather than hides its modern mechanical guts—its intake and exhaust systems for example—as it should, because it is devoted to the study of cutting-edge, experimental sciences. History had no place in the building program for this forward-looking structure.

To communicate architecturally, or to respond appropriately to a building's message, you must use or read its formal parts according to their associative meanings. This is not so that you can damn an architect who does not follow the grammatical niceties; rather, it is so that you can understand an architect even if he or she does not follow them. Architecture, as I have said, is like English, a highly flexible tool of communication. If an Italian mannerist architect like Giulio Romano lets drop a keystone in the courtyard at the Palazzo del Te in Mantua, or a contemporary deconstructionist like Frank Gehry shapes buildings like crumpled paper—as he did in the case of the Weisman Art Museum at the University of Minnesota in Minneapolis—these violations, respectively, of classical usage and reasonable form bespeak an experimental language as much as the "ungrammatical" poetry of Emily Dickinson or Gertrude Stein. This is not to say, of course, that all of these experiments are successful, or that we are obliged to like them very much.

The building blocks of language are vocabulary and grammar. The principal building block of architectural meaning is style, but materials, size, even location do play roles in how we interpret a building. We "read" marble differently than we read clapboards; a log cabin suggests a different mode of life from an alabaster castle. A log palace is an architectural as well as a verbal oxymoron; so is a short skyscraper, or an urban villa. A town house looks out of place in the countryside. In attempting to respond appropriately to a building program, the architect seeks a plan that is ser-

CIVIC CENTER

viceable, a structural system that is economically and technologically possible, and three-dimensional forms that are not only beautiful—in the eye of the architect and his or her client at least—but, usually, suggestive of the building type under consideration and its location.

I said above that a log palace is an oxymoron. Oxymorons exist, and they are not mute. The Great Camps of the Adirondacks, built of timbers on a palatial scale, derive their impact from such a juxtaposition of contradictory elements. On a work like his Civic Center in Portland, Oregon, Michael Graves used classical structural details decoratively and wrenched them out of scale.

He appropriated then enlarged a form suggesting a keystone and employed it in a trabeated building, thereby violating the rules that have long existed for classical design. As with verbal language, meaning in architecture derives from breaking as well as following rules.

But the value of the message sent by a building concerns the critic, not the writer of primers. I have in this elementary discussion of architecture consciously eschewed the question of quality. My intention has been to dissect a process, and to reveal its primary parts, not to judge the aesthetic achievement that results from the process. That would require a discussion of aesthetic theory as well as taste, and their histories, and that would go far beyond the scope of this modest grammar.

LEARNING THE LINGO

As we have seen, architecture is a language; buildings bear messages. Architecture has enriched our verbal language as well. Let us, finally, briefly consider the wonders of architectural terminology.

If you are going to analyze a building, you must know how to describe its parts. The parts of buildings have verbal equivalents. To name is to understand. Guessing at what an architectural element might be called, like assuming what a descriptive word might mean, can prove disastrous. Fortunately, learning the technical lingo can be surprisingly diverting. Sometimes when I am bored I curl up with a good architectural dictionary. Almost any dictionary will do, although I recommend a combination of Russell Sturgis's *Dictionary of Architecture*, *Webster's Third International*, the multi-volume *Oxford English Dictionary*, and Samuel Johnson's in the original mid-eighteenth-century edition. The last two especially will help you understand the origins or history of architectural terms, and that, too, can be as entertaining as it is instructive.

First, I search out and feast upon those strange-sounding words like *agrafe, bartizan, gazebo, machicolation, extrados, scantling, squint, skewback, jerkinhead, cyma recta,* and her backward sister, *cyma reversa*. What are these things? What does an architect draw when he designs a *quirk*, a *poppyhead*, an *astragal*, a *tringle*, or a *tail trimmer*? Why do buildings require *collar beams, labels, boltels, oriels,* or *merlons*? Or, for that matter, *puncheons, purlins,* or *put logs*? Do *sleepers* recline in *bed moldings*? What is a *fillet*, a *dado*, a *quarrel*, a *dingle*?

My advice is not to guess at the meaning of such fascinating words. Many sound a lot like what they are not. A *dental band*, for instance, is not a group of music-making orthodontists, but a series of small square blocks used to enrich a classical cornice. A *boltel* (for which, for reasons beyond my comprehension, Sturgis lists six different spellings, from *borstel* to *bottle*) is not a motel for boats (or a reform school or a container for liquids), but a round corner molding. A *colossal order* is not the meal of a trencherman, but a column, pier, or pilaster that vertically embraces more than one story. A *label* is not a sticker, but a projecting molding above an opening. Functionalist lexicographers will tell you it is there to shed water. It is in fact ornamental; it is there to trap shadows. A *poppyhead* is not a dope fiend, but a finial in the form of a flower. And a *merlon* is not a magician, but one of the solid intervals between the crenels of a battlemented parapet. (You must now look up *crenel*.) The definitions are as wonderful as the words!

Some of these terms sound so strange that you know the minute you encounter them that you should head for *Webster's*. No one in polite company has the nerve to guess aloud at the meaning of *skewback* or *jerkinhead*, but a dictionary will reassure you that the former is a course of masonry, a stone, or an iron plate having an inclined face against which rest the lowest voussoirs of a segmental arch. And that will be perfectly clear as soon as you look up *voussoirs* and *segmental arch*. *Jerkinhead*, believe it or not, is also in *Webster's*. It is "the hipped part of a roof which is hipped only for part of its height leaving a truncated gable." That's almost poetry! An *agrafe* is a hook used to hold together the stones in a wall. (In a saloon it is that wire gadget used to secure the cork in a champagne bottle.) And *machicolation*, mellifluous *machicolation*, refers to an opening between two corbels that support a projecting cornice. Through it you could shoot arrows or bolts from a

crossbow, or pour boiling oil on besieging enemies and other un-
wanted guests.

According to the dictionaries, parts of buildings can possess the
most violent-sounding afflictions. They can be *battered, stopped,
imbricated, bosselated, vermiculated, cantoned, denticulated,
pulvinated,* or, horror of horrors, apparently, *gadrooned.* How
would you like to be *bosselated, pulvinated,* or *gadrooned*? The
very words make me wince.

A little perusal of a dictionary will ease the phonetic fright. A
pilaster or building that is *cantoned* has not been exiled to a Chinese restaurant. Rather, it has exterior corners decorated with projecting members. A *denticulated* cornice has not been gnawed
but enlivened with *dentils.* To be *gadrooned,* if you are an architectural detail, means that you are decorated with convex curves;
it is the opposite of *fluting. Bosselated* is a gift from the French
meaning that a vault is covered with *bosses.* And a *battered* wall
is not a social problem, like a battered child or a battered wife; it
is, rather, a surface that slopes inward as it rises to give stability or
the effect of it. How reassuring.

Most of these words sound vaguely plausible as terms you
might use when referring to a building or its parts, but there are
other nouns in the architectural vocabulary at which we can only
stare in disbelief. If we can credit the lexicographers, there are to
be found in or on buildings the following motley assortment:
lutherans, rabbets, crickets, and *running dogs; barges* and *barefoot studs; soldiers* and *bosses; naves; eyebrows, diapers,* and
quoins. Do such things really pertain to a building? Or is this riot
of nouns and adjectives the lexicographer's idea of sport? Surely a
barefoot stud is some country lover? Who could mistake the
meaning of *running dog, rabbet, diaper,* or *soldier*? A *barge* is a
boat, right? The *boss* is the grump I work for. A *nave* is a mis-

spelled rascal; a *quoin* is legal tender however it is written. *Crickets* are chirping bugs. Lucky the homeowner who has one on the hearth, but does he want them elsewhere in the house? To the delight of the architectural critic or historian, who in speaking or writing seeks to make buildings come to life, these are in fact legitimate technical terms.

On a sloping roof a *cricket* is a false roof that directs water around an obstacle such as a chimney. A *boss* is an ornamental knob or projection covering the intersection of ribs in a vault or ceiling. A *barge* is the often elaborately ornamental board along the raking edge of a gable. It is apparently a corruption of *verge*, which is also used at times. A *running dog* is a continuous wave ornament found in classical architecture. *Quoins* are the boards, bricks, or stones at the corners of a building that are emphasized in order to frame a facade. The word was appropriated from the printshop, where a quoin is used to lock type into place.

In older heavy timber construction a *rabbet*, which is a corruption of *rebate*, is a mortise or notch cut into one structural member to receive the end of another. A *barefoot stud* is a vertical wood framing member, a two-by-four say, that is set up and fastened to the plate with nails rather than with mortise and tenon. It was a local American term that obviously had its origin in the second quarter of the nineteenth century when lightweight or balloon framing began to replace the earlier and heavier pegged-timber frame. With this definition I have resorted to historical explanation; or, rather, I have progressed into the world of etymology, the study of the origin and historical development of words.

These colorful terms come into English from a variety of sources, especially Greek, Latin, and French, or they are native born. Some come from the art of building, some from the sciences, and some come from far outside either art or science.

Meaning may remain more or less constant even when forms are somewhat altered, but some words gain broadened definitions through travel. Some retain their forms while assuming new meanings, and some carry constant meanings through changing forms. If you would like to increase your understanding of architecture and its history, improve your vocabulary, and boost your measure of entertainment, you must now enter upon the etymological path. You must become a student of evolving linguistic forms. Here are some examples of the game.

If you live in a house with a high roof, the chances are good that you have *lutherans* coming out of the attic. A *lutheran* in architectural usage is simply a dormer, a vertical opening in a sloping roof, usually having a roof of its own. *Dormer* derives from the fact that an attic frequently served as sleeping quarters, or a *dormitory*. Does, then, a *lutheran* light a sectarian attic? No. The word is nondenominational. Commonly spelled *luthern* in modern English dictionaries, it is a direct borrowing from the French, for whom a dormer is a *lucarne*. When in the seventeenth century the English came strongly under the influence of French architecture, writers like the diarists Samuel Pepys and John Evelyn took over the word whole while softening the *c*.

Lutheran is simple borrowing, and easy enough to follow. It plays in the etymological kindergarten. What about *piazza*?

When our Victorian forebears relaxed on a summer's eve, like as not they took air on the front porch, the veranda, or, as many called it, the piazza. The piazza? Isn't that the Italian word for an urban open space? How did the term for a civic square in southern Europe come to mean an American front porch? The answer combines social, architectural, and linguistic history.

When the English gentry in the Renaissance took the grand tour through Europe to the Mediterranean, they usually entered Italy

from the Ligurian Sea through the Tuscan port of Livorno, a name
they Anglicized to *Leghorn*. The center of Leghorn is occupied by
the Piazza Grande, an urban open space surrounded by a classical arcade and focused on a church. When, early in the seventeenth century, London began to absorb the architectural and
urban-planning lessons of Italian classicism, the square at Covent
Garden in London was designed by the architect Inigo Jones in
the image of the Piazza Grande at Leghorn. Defined by arcades, it
was anchored on the little church of Saint Paul's. With characteristic eccentricity, the English applied the term *piazza* not to the
square as a whole, but to the arcades surrounding it. In the late
seventeenth century, then, you might have said of a friend that
she lived in one of the piazzas in Covent Garden. By the mid-
eighteenth century Samuel Johnson could define a piazza as simply "a walk under a roof supported by pillars."

This transference of meaning from center to periphery came to
the New World with English immigrant architects in the late eighteenth century, and it survived into the nineteenth. Then, across
time and the Atlantic, the Italian word for civic square became the
term used by Anglo-Saxons for the ubiquitous American front
porch, whose roof was often supported by arches. And, according
to the *Oxford English Dictionary*, possible anglicized forms of the
word include *piazzaed, piazzaless, piazzetta*, and *piazzian*. Such
is the elasticity of language!

Let's end with one more example of the migrating meaning of
words. If *fornication* comes up in conversation with an architect,
the reference may not be to Deuteronomy 5:18. Fornication does
not only refer to "when two vnweddyde haue misdoun," as an
early fourteenth-century commentator put it so gently. Sturgis defines the term as "the process, or act, of covering with a vault." In
Latin a vault is a *fornix*. So how do we get our usual meaning of

the word? In ancient Rome, prostitutes frequented the vaulted arcades surrounding the Colosseum.

I hope, finally, to have convinced you of the instructional and even entertainment value of the study of architectural terminology. If you are now reaching for a copy of Sturgis, Johnson, the *OED, Webster's*, or whatever reference work you have on hand, my mission has been accomplished. Having pointed the route, I can leave you to your journey.

GLOSSARY

Words in *italics* are defined in this Glossary.

ADDITIVE PLAN   The disjointed, accumulative, and often asymmetrical arrangement of the discretely formed areas composing certain buildings. Such a *plan* usually underlies a *picturesque* design.

ARCADE   A row of *arches.*

ARCH   In an *arcuated* structural system, a curved unit of construction, usually of masonry and usually composed of wedge-shaped blocks called *voussoirs,* spanning an opening between upright supports.

ARCUATED STRUCTURE   A construction of *arches, arcades,* and *vaults.*

ASHLAR MASONRY   Masonry formed of square or rectangular stones. Random ashlar displays interrupted vertical and horizontal joints, while horizontal or layered ashlar has interrupted vertical but continuous horizontal joints.

ASTYLAR   A wall or building without *columns* or *pilasters.*

BALLOON FRAME   As opposed to traditional *heavy timber construction,* a light-weight wooden structural system introduced in the United States in the early nineteenth century in which the basic unit is a machine-sawn two-by-four-inch upright *stud* repeated on sixteen-inch centers.

BAROQUE   In art history, a style prevalent in Europe during the seventeenth century. It is often characterized by abundant curves and exuberant ornament.

BARREL VAULT   Overhead covering in the form of a horizontal half-cylinder.

BASILICA   A church with *nave* and side aisles.

BATTERED   In architecture, a term for a wall or *pier* that slopes backward as it rises from the ground.

BEAM   In a *trabeated* structural system, a straight, horizontal member spanning between two supporting uprights; a *lintel.*

BENDING MOMENT   "Moment" is the property by which a force causes a body to rotate about a point or line. In the "bending moment" that rotation causes flexing in a *beam* or other structural member.

BUILDING PROGRAM   The written or oral statement of the needs a building is intended to satisfy.

BUTTRESS   A structural member counterbalancing the diagonal thrust of an *arch* or *vault.*

BYZANTINE ARCHITECTURE   A style of building spanning from the fourth century onward and centered on present-day Istanbul. It is characterized by the multiplicity of domical *vaults* that are often supported by *pendentives.*

CANTILEVER   In a *trabeated* structure, a *beam* supported at one end only or balanced on a central support with both ends free.

CHANGE ORDER   Official authorization to alter an architectural design after the contract has been signed and work has begun.

CHIAROSCURO   The play of light and shadow.

CLASSICISM   In architectural history, the styles of building in ancient Greece and Rome and their descendants in the Western tradition. The basic language of classicism is embodied in the five orders: *Tuscan, Doric, Ionic, Corinthian,* and *Composite.*

COLUMN   An upright support that is round in *plan.*

COMMON BOND   Brickwork in which every fifth or sixth course consists of headers, or bricks placed perpendicular to the length of the wall. The other courses contain stretchers, or bricks that run parallel to the wall.

COMPOSITE ORDER   A Roman addition to the Greek canon, it is the most delicate of the orders of classical architecture. Its capital combines *Ionic* volutes with the *Corinthian* acanthus.

COMPRESSION   A force that pushes. One of two opposing forces in a building, the other being *tension.* The two must be balanced if the building is to stand.

CORINTHIAN ORDER   The most elaborate of the Greek orders of architecture, it is characterized by slender proportions and conventionalized acanthus leaf capitals.

CORNICE   The projecting decorative profile at the top of a wall.

DADO The skirting above the base of a wall.

DEAD LOAD The weight of a structure and its inert contents.

DIVISIVE PLAN The design of a building in which the individual areas seem subdivided from a larger whole and are usually arranged symmetrically. Such a plan often underlies a classical or neoclassical structure.

DOME A *vault* in the shape of a hemisphere.

DORIC ORDER The simplest of the Greek orders of architecture, it is characterized by sturdy proportions and simple, spreading capitals.

EARLY CHRISTIAN ARCHITECTURE The buildings, primarily churches, of the waning western Roman empire from the fourth to the sixth century.

ELEVATION In architectural graphics, the representation on a vertical plane of the exterior or interior walls of a building.

ENDOSKELETAL STRUCTURE In an animal or a building, a *structure* hidden within an outer skin.

ENGAGED COLUMN A half- or three-quarter-round *column* attached to a wall.

ENGLISH BOND Brickwork with alternating courses of headers (bricks perpendicular to the length of the wall) and stretchers (bricks placed lengthwise to the wall).

EXOSKELETAL STRUCTURE In an animal or a building, a *structure* exposed on the exterior.

FIRMITAS In Latin, "firmness" or "stability," one of the three essential components of architecture named by the ancient writer Vitruvius. The other components are *Utilitas* and *Venustas.*

FLEMISH BOND Brickwork in which each course is laid in alternating headers (bricks set perpendicular to the length of the wall) and stretchers (bricks set lengthwise to the wall).

FOOTING The underground spread foundation on which a building rests.

FOOTPRINT In architects' lingo, a *plan.*

FORMAL An architectural form that is balanced, symmetrical, and regular; the opposite of *picturesque.*

GOTHIC ARCHITECTURE The predominent architecture of Europe from the thirteenth to the sixteenth century. Its most characteristic feature is the *pointed arch.*

GREEK ARCHITECTURE In this work, the buildings of the classical period in ancient Greece. Its most characteristic feature is its *trabeated* structure.

GROIN VAULT Usually a *vault* composed of the perpendicular intersection of two *barrel vaults.* The line of intersection, the groin, may be plain or emphasized by a rib.

HEAVY TIMBER CONSTRUCTION   A pre-industrial system of wooden building in which the members are joined by *mortises* and *tenons* held together with *trunnels.*

HORSESHOE ARCH   An *arch* whose curve continues beyond the semicircle. Commonly found in Islamic architecture.

IONIC ORDER   The second of the three orders of classical Greek architecture. It is recognized by the volutes of its capital.

ISLAMIC DECORATION   In architecture, ornamentation that is characteristically intricate and geometric.

LINTEL   In a *trabeated* structural system, a *beam.*

LIVE LOAD   The stress imposed on a *structure* by occupants, traffic, wind, and other shifting forces.

LUNETTE   A small round or arched window penetrating an overhead *vault.*

MECHANICAL SYSTEM   Any or all of the building services provided by heating, ventilating, electricity, plumbing, and so forth.

MODULE   An arbitrary unit of measure used in building design and construction.

MORTISE   In *heavy timber construction,* the cavity or recess cut into one member to receive the *tenon* of another. Mortise and tenon are held together with *trunnels.*

NAVE   The area of a church on the axis of the main altar that is intended for the use of the congregation.

NEOCLASSICISM European and American architecture of the late eighteenth and early nineteenth centuries. It is characterized by restrained ornament and the strict use of the orders.

OGEE ARCH A *pointed arch* whose sides are S-curves.

PENDENTIVE A vault in the form of a spherical triangle that bridges between a square in *plan* and the circle at the bottom of a *dome*.

PICTURESQUE In this work, architectural forms that are asymmetrical, irregular, additive, colorful, and dynamic. It is the opposite of *formal*.

PIER An upright support that is square in *plan*.

PILASTER A thin *pier* that projects from a wall.

PILOTIS Heavy uprights, usually of *reinforced concrete*, used to raise a building off the ground.

PLAN The diagram of the horizontal arrangement of spaces in a building; or, the horizontal section of any part of a building.

PLATE GLASS High quality, usually large, sheets of polished glass.

POINTED ARCH An *arch* with a pointed crown which characterizes the *Gothic* style.

POST AND BEAM See *Post and lintel*.

POST AND LINTEL   A structural system of uprights supporting horizontal *beams* that span the space between them. Also called *trabeated* or *post and beam*.

PRIMARY SPACES The most important rooms in a building.

REINFORCED CONCRETE   A structural material composed of concrete (a compound of cement, aggregates, and water) and *steel* reinforcing bars, or rebars.

RENAISSANCE ARCHITECTURE   The revival of ancient Roman classical building style that began in Italy in the fifteenth century and spread throughout Europe by the nineteenth.

RISER The vertical face between the treads of a stair.

ROCOCO ARCHITECTURE   An early eighteenth-century style, mainly French, characterized by lightness of color and form and an excess of decoration.

ROMAN ARCHITECTURE In this work, the classical buildings of ancient Rome. Its most characteristic feature is its *arcuated* structure.

ROMANESQUE ARCHITECTURE   European building of the eleventh and twelfth centuries characterized by massive walls, heavy *barrel vaults*, and round-arched openings.

SCALE The relationship of one part of a building to another, or the relationship of a whole or part of a building to the human figure.

SECONDARY SPACES   Those areas of a building, such as stairs, hallways, or restrooms, that make the *primary spaces* usable.

SECTION   In architectural graphics, the presentation of a building as it would look if cut by a vertical plane. The section usually shows the structural system as well as the roof, the superimposed floors and their connectors, and interior elevations.

SHEAR STRESS   Shear is a fracture along parallel planes. Shear stress is the force per unit area of cross section necessary to produce shear.

SITE   A building's location; the land on which a building stands.

SKYSCRAPER   An urban commercial building type of exaggerated vertical proportions usually achieved by the use of *steel* or *reinforced concrete* frame construction. The skyscraper first appeared in some cities of the United States in the fourth quarter of the nineteenth century.

SPACE   In architecture, the two- or three-dimensional extent of a room or rooms. The architect can manipulate the character of a space by size, shape, scale, color, lighting, and so forth.

STASIS   A state of equilibrium among opposing forces. In architecture, the opposing forces are *tension* and *compression.*

STATICS   The area of mechanics concerned with forces acting on bodies in equilibrium.

STEEL An alloy of iron and carbon.

STRUCTURE The armature or supporting framework of a building.

STUD In building construction, one of many vertical two-by-four-inch wooden members in a *balloon frame*.

STYLOBATE The base or platform on which *columns* rest.

SUSPENSION STRUCTURE A structural system in which *tension* cables carry the overhead load to balancing *compression* members.

TENON In *heavy timber construction*, the reduced section at the end of a member, or tongue, that fits into the cavity, or *mortise*, of another member in order to form a joint. Mortise and tenon are held together with *trunnels*.

TENSION A force that pulls or stretches. One of the two opposing forces in a building, the other being *compression*. The two must be balanced if the building is to stand.

TRABEATED STRUCTURE A system of construction using upright posts, *columns*, or *piers* supporting horizontal *beams* or *lintels* that span the space between them. Also called *post and lintel* or *post and beam*.

TRUNNEL From the word "treenail"; a wooden peg used to secure the *mortise* and *tenon* joints in *heavy timber construction*.

TRUSS A structural unit composed of a combination of members placed horizontally, vertically, or diagonally that acts as a *beam* in spanning large distances.

TUSCAN ORDER A Roman addition to the Greek canon, it is the simplest and sturdiest of all the orders of classical architecture.

UTILITAS In Latin, "utility" or "function," one of the three essential components of architecture named by the ancient writer Vitruvius. The other components are *Firmitas* and *Venustas*.

VAULT A curved overhead covering, usually of masonry.

VENUSTAS In Latin, "beauty," one of the three essential components of architecture named by the ancient writer Vitruvius. The other components are *Firmitas* and *Utilitas*.

VICTORIAN ARCHITECTURE A building style popular in England during the reign of Queen Victoria (1840-1901), it is characterized by picturesque forms inspired by medieval buildings.

VOUSSOIR A wedge-shaped block used to build an *arch*.

WIND BRACING In *trabeated construction*, the diagonal members used to counteract the lateral stress caused by wind pressure.

FURTHER READING

There are many books on the general topic of architecture. A few basic ones that expand on the introductory material presented in this volume are listed below. They are recommended for reading at the next level.

Abercrombie, Stanley. *Architecture as Art*. New York: Van Nostrand Reinhold, 1984.

Banham, Reyner. *The Architecture of the Well-Tempered Environment*. Chicago: University of Chicago Press, 1984.

Conway, Hazel, and Rowan Roenisch. *Understanding Architecture*. London: Routledge, 1994.

Frankl, Paul. *Principles of Architectural History*. Translated and edited by James F. O'Gorman. Cambridge, Mass.: MIT Press, 1968.

Gauldie, Sinclair. *Architecture*. London: Oxford University Press, 1969.

Mitchell, William J. *The Logic of Architecture*. Cambridge, Mass.: MIT Press, 1990.

Rasmussen, Steen Eiler. *Experiencing Architecture*. Translated by Eve Wendt. London: Chapman and Hall, 1959.

Roth, Leland. *Understanding Architecture*. New York: Icon Editions, 1993.

Salvadori, Mario. *Building: The Fight Against Gravity*. New York: Athenaeum, 1979.

Vitruvius Pollio. *On Architecture*. Cambridge, Mass.: Harvard University Press (Loeb Classical Library), 1983–85.

INDEX